D1460836

P. 43. Redundacy.

EMPLOYEE
RELATIONS

**Elizabeth
Aylott**

KoganPage

LONDON PHILADELPHIA NEW DELHI

First published in Great Britain and the United States in 2014 by Kogan Page Limited
Reprinted 2014, 2015

Apart from any fair dealing for the purposes of research or private study, or criticism or review, as permitted under the Copyright, Designs and Patents Act 1988, this publication may only be reproduced, stored or transmitted, in any form or by any means, with the prior permission in writing of the publishers, or in the case of reprographic reproduction in accordance with the terms and licences issued by the CLA. Enquiries concerning reproduction outside these terms should be sent to the publishers at the undermentioned addresses:

2nd Floor, 45 Gee Street
London EC1V 3RS
United Kingdom
www.koganpage.com

1518 Walnut Street, Suite 1100
Philadelphia PA 19102
USA

4737/23 Ansari Road
Daryaganj
New Delhi 110002
India

© Elizabeth Aylott, 2014

The right of Elizabeth Aylott to be identified as the author of this work has been asserted by her in accordance with the Copyright, Designs and Patents Act 1988.

ISBN   978 0 7494 6976 4
E-ISBN   978 0 7494 6977 1

British Library Cataloguing-in-Publication Data

A CIP record for this book is available from the British Library.

Library of Congress Cataloging-in-Publication Data

Aylott, Elizabeth.
  Employee relations / Elizabeth Aylott.
    pages cm
  ISBN 978-0-7494-6976-4 – ISBN 978-0-7494-6977-1 (e-ISBN)   1. Industrial relations.   I. Title.
  HD6958.5.A95 2014
  658.3–dc23

                                                                                    2013037263

Typeset by Graphicraft Limited, Hong Kong
Printed and bound by CPI Group (UK) Ltd, Croydon, CR0 4YY

Dedication

With love to my girls; along with others
I am privileged to share some very small part
of your lives as you build your future.

To Alice, Rebecca, Hannah,
Ella and Maija.

CONTENTS

ABOUT THE AUTHOR

Liz Aylott is based at BPP where, as a member of the faculty Business School, she lectures on HRM and business degrees, and Master's level programmes. For 10 years she has also lectured on the business degrees and the CIPD programmes at levels three, five and seven at Farnborough College of Technology. She has provided a range of training programmes for individuals and clients and advice for businesses, ranging from a series of courses to introduce a new performance management system to career development and outplacement workshops.

Liz has a passion for developing expertise at all levels, for those embarking on a new career or for more experienced professionals, and for making learning accessible to all. For example, she has enjoyed coaching individual students through a range of business-based NVQ and Apprenticeships at a variety of different businesses, from large multinational corporations to small businesses. Whilst possessing an enthusiasm for facilitating and supporting employees to build on their strengths, she also has enjoyed the ability to provide advice as necessary, in particular for small businesses as they develop their HRM practice.

She has a broad interest in HRM but with an emphasis on employee voice, perceptions of justice and fairness, supporting HRM in SMEs and also employee absence and poor performance. She has written Case Studies on Employment Law for the CIPD and a Study Manual for Employment Relations Diploma Level 5, prepared for the Association of Business Executives and produced by BPP Media to support students completing this qualification.

Her primary areas of expertise are Employee Relations and Employment Law, an interest formed when she practised as a qualified HR Manager over 15 years ago. This interest has been developed from experience in a range of sectors, from the NHS (where she first practised as a physiotherapist), to the charitable sector (provision for disabled adults) and manufacturing industry (contact lens manufacture). This experience of being an employee (at the production line, either as a physiotherapist providing a service or as a lecturer developing education), of being a Line Manager, a Senior Manager and HRM professional has held her in good stead.

Introduction

Employee Relations

The only exposure the general public have to Employee Relations is the coverage of strikes and protests, as Trade Union members put voice to their disputes. The public listen to the rhetoric of both parties and the distorted arguments, and they form their own view based on these arguments and any disruption they have had to their own lives.

The most recent concerted action that the public would remember is when workers protested against the austerity measures taken by European Governments. Workers in Italy and Portugal, Spain and Greece went on strike in November 2012, whilst in the UK, where the law restricts secondary action, and therefore a general strike is more difficult, workers demonstrated in London. Some of the public would have supported the protest against Government austerity measures, having felt the impact of these measures on their own lives, as their own employers cut pay or made redundancies, while other members of the public would have supported the Government's measures.

In the UK, for example, the National Union of Teachers and the NASUWT took strike action in June 2013 over changes to pensions, performance-related pay, later retirement and increased workloads. As I write this, more strikes are threatened for autumn 2013. The view of the public will again depend on their experiences and values, their political affiliation and their view of Trade Unions, Management and central Government.

However, they may not see that Employee Relations is much more than the relationship between Trade Unions, their membership, employers and Government, and that Employee Relations refers to the employee's own relationship with their employer, through their contract, their Line Manager and Human Resources.

Employee Relations is fundamental to Human Resources as it brings the formal agreement, the employment contract, to life. As HR professionals we recognize the need to understand employment law, but it is only there because of the challenges of ensuring a good employment relationship. We might train and develop employees but we will not get the best out of them without a good employment relationship. We might try to pay them well, but again it is good employment relationships that will get the best out of employees.

This book helps explain why Employee Relations is important and how to build that relationship effectively.

Aims of the book

This book is set out to be a very practical guide to Employee Relations so that HR professionals are able to easily access information to guide them in best practice. It is important that we have the resources at our fingertips to gain credibility with managers, enabling us to make a difference, so that we are able to develop our careers and Employee Relations specialists and HR generalists are given greater recognition. So the book has been written to meet the needs of practitioners who are relatively new to the Employee Relations specialism, or those with an HR generalist remit.

This book also attempts to provide a foundation for those of us completing the Level 5 Intermediate Certificate in HRM or the Level 5 Apprenticeship scheme. It has been written to meet the range of learning outcomes for both these qualifications: the learning outcomes of both CIPD qualifications are given in Table 0.1. It can also support degree-level students who may wish to use a very practically-based book to understand Employee Relations. Whilst this book has not been written to support Level 7's academic rigour it does have the basics for those with little Employee Relations experience taking an Employee Relations module. It has been written to provide a good basic understanding and is a good introductory text to a complex and valuable area of Human Resources.

It is important to stress that this book should be read together with its companion book, **HR Fundamentals: Employment Law** (Aylott, 2014). Employee Relations cannot be practised without knowledge of the law, and particularly the legislation and case law that refers to discipline and grievances, which is included in this book.

TABLE 0.1 Cross mapping of content of CIPD Level 5 courses

CIPD Learning Outcomes Intermediate Level Certificate in HRM	CIPD Learning Outcomes for Level 5 Diploma in applied HRM – Higher Apprenticeship	Topics	Found in
1. Understand competing approaches that contextualize contemporary developments in employment relations.	1. Understand theoretical approaches to employment relations.	Unitarism and pluralism, balance of power, economic and psychological contracts	Ch1
		Nature of contemporary work society	Conclusion
2. Understand contemporary labour market trends and data.		The labour market, employee and employer interests and different forms of employment	Ch1
		Changing patterns of workforce diversity	Conclusion
3. Understand the main sources of employment relations legislation.		Legislation covering agency part-time workers, fair reasons for dismissal	Ch1
		Protecting employee rights, an ethical perspective	Ch2
		Grievance procedures, constructive dismissal, discipline procedure, poor performance, collective bargaining, industrial action	Ch4

TABLE 0.1 *continued*

CIPD Learning Outcomes Intermediate Level Certificate in HRM	CIPD Learning Outcomes for Level 5 Diploma in applied HRM – Higher Apprenticeship	Topics	Found in
4. Understand the role of the parties that affect the management of employment relations.	2. Understand the roles of key parties involved in employment relations.	Key contributors at National, European and International levels	Ch1
		The cost of individual and collective conflict	Ch2
		The choice of Union representation	Ch3
		Union recognition	Ch4
		Trade union decline	Conclusion
5. Understand contemporary developments in employee involvement and participation.	3. Understand different models of employee representation.	Defining involvement, participation and employee voice and communication methods.	Ch1
		Involvement, participation and their role in organizational performance	Ch2
		Making strategic decisions on EIP methods	Ch3
		Improving downward communication	Ch4
		Designing EIP Schemes	Ch5
		Employee representation and voice – from the WERS Survey 2011	Ch6

TABLE 0.1 *continued*

CIPD Learning Outcomes Intermediate Level Certificate in HRM	CIPD Learning Outcomes for Level 5 Diploma in applied HRM – Higher Apprenticeship	Topics	Found in
6. Understand different forms of conflict behaviour and dispute resolution.	4. Understand different forms of conflict behaviour and dispute resolution.	The basis of conflict in an organization and third party arbitration and conciliation	Ch1
		The role of conflict in innovation and how the Employee Relations professional can support conflict management	Ch2
		Strategic decisions on conflict and dispute resolution methods	Ch3
		Discipline and grievance mechanisms and the process of industrial action	Ch4
		Mediation schemes. How to prepare for and carry out a grievance meeting. The skills needed to carry out investigations. How to carry out interviews and listen actively. How to prepare for collective bargaining and negotiation. How to minimize the effects of industrial action on the employer.	Ch5
		Discontent in the workforce – from the WERS survey 2011, measuring the employment relationship.	Ch6

Structure of the book

This book takes us on a journey, with the first three chapters providing the foundations of knowledge which the last three chapters apply in practice. It starts in the first three chapters by giving us a definition of what Employee Relations actually is and its importance to business and individuals, and goes on to link Employee Relations to business and HR strategy, finally identifying how the different aspects of Employee Relations work. The last two chapters are very practical and review the skills we will need to carry out Employee Relations and how we can measure them.

Each chapter uses a minimum of technical terminology, but it also needs to meet the requirements of students at Level 5. Where possible case studies have been used to illustrate and give examples of practice, and question-naires used to help HR professionals apply what has been mentioned in the chapter to their own experience or their own organization.

In Chapter 1 we define and describe Employee Relations and see how it differs from the more traditional Industrial Relations, introducing the key organizations involved in Employee Relations, both nationally and interna-tionally. We look at the role of the psychological contract and power in the employment relationship and the causes of conflict. This chapter acts as the theoretical foundation for the chapters that follow.

In Chapter 2 we stress the need for Employee Relations, its role in ensuring that employees' rights are protected and that employers behave both legally and ethically. We also look at the role Employee Involvement and Parti-cipation takes on individual and organizational performance.

In Chapter 3 we start by making sure we have a fundamental understanding of business and HR strategy before reviewing the strategic choices those leading Employee Relations might make. In the recent past Employee Rela-tions has been reactive, unplanned and rarely integrated into the mission, culture and goals of the organization. This chapter amends this to support a more professional approach to Employee Relations.

In Chapter 4 we explain how different aspects of Employee Relations work in practice. We specifically review downward communication methods before examining what is required of a grievance and discipline procedure and shedding light on the difficult concept of constructive dismissal. When we examine collective Employee Relations we describe the process of Union recognition and explain the law surrounding industrial action and action short of strike action.

In Chapter 5 we focus more on the practical skills needed to plan and implement Employee Relations. When looking at involving Trade Unions we discuss the more contemporary approach to collective Employee Relations with a review of partnership working with Trade Unions. We also cover the skills required to support those who are investigating a grievance and how to manage a grievance meeting. We particularly focus on mediation schemes within the workplace, encouraged by the Government as one of the alternative dispute mechanisms that reduce the need for costly Employment Tribunals. We look at the need for negotiation skills when bargaining with Trade Unions and how to manage if your employer is subject to a strike.

In Chapter 6 we examine how we might measure employee relations or to be more accurate, the employment relationship. It is difficult for employers to assess the employment relationship as this is influenced by a range of variables. However this chapter explains how an in-house survey could be designed and how other measures, such as employee turnover, can provide additional data. It also looks at the first findings of the Workplace Employment Relations Survey conducted in 2011 (Van Wanrooy et al, 2013) which provides information on a sample of companies in the UK.

PART ONE

FUNDAMENTALS

What is Employee Relations?

01

INTRODUCTION

Employee Relations is concerned with the management and maintenance of the employment relationship, essentially how management
and the employees of any organization interact. In this chapter we
will look at the development of Employee Relations and explore:

- the difference between Industrial Relations and Employee
  Relations;
- the employment relationship and psychological contract;
- the role of power in the employment relationship;
- key contributors at national, European and international levels;
- involvement, participation and employee voice;
- the basis of conflict within the organization;
- the end of the employment relationship.

Background: Industrial Relations and Employee Relations

What are Industrial Relations and Employee Relations?

Industrial Relations is the term used to describe the relationship between
employer and employee collectively through the Trade Union, acting as a
collective voice for employees.

In the UK it was in such a situation that Industrial Relations had its roots in 1875 when six agricultural workers, known as the Tolpuddle Martyrs, attempting to form a Trade Union, were arrested and transported to Australia. Today there exists in the UK a structure of Unions available to represent employees, and employment legislation supporting good employee and employer relations. In different countries the role of Trade Unionism and the scope of employment legislation vary, dependent on the history and culture of that country. In the majority of countries the industrial landscape has changed, and in recent years there has been a reduction in membership of Unions, with OECD (Organisation for Economic Co-operation and Development) countries reporting a decline in membership from 20.8 per cent of population in 1999 to 17.5 per cent of population in 2010 (OECD, 2010).

However, Employee Relations is the relationship between the employee and the employer, through representation if it is available, but often without a Trade Union. We, as HR professionals and Line Managers, act as representatives of the employer, and often an employee's main relationship with the employer will be through their Line Manager. As with all relationships, communication between both parties is important, but with the imbalance of power between the employer and employee frequently managers communicate downward to employees, with less time given to listen to employees' contributions. Yet if we do allow employees to contribute and involve them they are likely to be motivated and their suggestions can support business performance.

So, Employee Relations concerns communication with employees and also the involvement and participation of employees, but at times the relationship has problems that need to be resolved. Employee Relations also covers the conflict between employer and employee (and in fact between employees), and the discipline and grievance procedures support the employer in managing these disputes. If the employee is represented by a Trade Union they may seek their help to represent and guide them at a formal discipline or grievance hearing. It may be that the Trade Union negotiates with the employer, and if the outcome of the negotiation is not acceptable to the Union, there may be circumstances where it decides that it must take industrial action. If we have Employee Relations experience we may be involved in the negotiation or need to support Line Managers who may be attempting to continue work as usual during the strike.

All this needs to be carried out within the law, and this is our main concern as HR professionals. We might find it difficult to ensure that the relationship between Line Managers and employees meets legal requirements; this is not under our control. Yet we might well find ourselves at an Employment Tribunal supporting the employer despite the fact that a Line Manager has not listened to our advice.

In context – the labour market

The labour market provides the arrangement through which workers can interact with employers to gain jobs and to agree payment for these jobs. Within this marketplace, potential employees seek work and employers seek to fill their vacancies. This market enables competition to attract employees to the best offer, with supply and demand of employees moderating the wages. The state of the labour market can be evaluated by measures such as unemployment and wage levels.

Employers need to ensure that their organizations make a profit and so need to obtain appropriately skilled workers who will work efficiently and effectively for the lowest wage possible. Employees need work that provides at least a living wage to ensure that they and their families have the money to meet their debts. However, individuals are motivated also by the social identity and social contact that is provided by work, along with the recognition and status that employment can bring. Finally there is also the opportunity for self-development through training or the challenge of promotion (Maslow, 1987).

Within the labour market, regulation is provided to protect the employee and according to Dibben, Klerck and Wood (2011: 12) to *'encourage specific behavioural patterns (that is, encouraging employers and employees to engage in certain behaviours) through the imposition of costs and rewards'*. In the UK legislation is formulated nationally as statutes and through case law, but is also influenced by international bodies such as the European Union, and internationally by membership of the United Nations and the International Labour Organization.

The extent of market regulation is important in the ability of a country to attract foreign investment. If it is easier to recruit and dismiss employees than in other countries then a multinational corporation (MNC) may look favourably on this location. If the need for employee consultation and restrictions on working time are demanding, the MNC may be dissuaded from investing. The MNC will balance the costs of regulation, labour costs and other operational requirements to support their decision.

An example of a decision on location of a business site is Hoover in 1993. Production was expanded in Hoover's Scottish plant and the production site in the French town of Dijon was closed. Despite discussions with the French employees, the Scottish employees had greater flexibility in employment law, in particular the pension regulation and working time regulation that made it financially more viable for Hoover to choose the Scottish location (EIRR, 1993).

It may be argued that a country should have limited employment legislation, employers should be able to hire and fire at will and labour costs should be low. Whilst such conditions may attract external investment it would not protect employees. Governments have to balance the needs of the employees for employment protection and the restrictions that the laws they pass have on the market.

Finally, globalization also means that employees take assignments all over the world. These assignments are not new jobs with new employers, but roles within a single MNC which has work locations worldwide. The membership of the European Union enables employees to easily move and work between different EU countries. Outside of this region, employees become subject to the immigration policies of the country they wish to enter. The case study below describes global roles at HSBC.

So the labour market has extended widely in recent years. Whilst for many potential employees the driving distance from home gives the extent of their labour market and for others with good rail networks, the labour market may extend to a UK region, increasingly there is a wider global labour market. The following case study illustrates the wider labour market and looks at what HSBC has to offer for those employees willing and able to take a global role.

CASE STUDY   Global working at HSBC

HSBC offer an International Manager Programme for newly qualified graduates. According to HSBC *'our IMs build up a portfolio of global management and banking skills, which they develop from a range of challenging assignments. These could be in any one of the 87 countries and territories in which we operate, across both developed and emerging markets'*. After a month of training IMs will be posted to a global role and will be assigned a new role every 18 months. They are expected to continue to offer global mobility throughout their career.

One IM, a Channel Sales Manager in Kazakhstan, describes the experience:

> *My role in Kazakhstan has evolved significantly in the year that I have been here. I moved out here at short notice to assist with the acquisition and integration of the RBS retail bank and portfolio. This involved the transfer of 45,000 customers and 450 staff in a relatively short time frame of six months. As we had a small team in Kazakhstan, the role has meant that I have had exposure to many different areas, including valuation of the business, writing business cases, understanding of tax issues, setting up new products, briefing senior management, staff and customer communications, and even on occasion providing an extra resource at the branches during the weekend!*

> *Now that the integration is over, I am responsible for creating a unified approach and managing direct banking, which involves the call centre, ATMs, internet and SMS banking. It's a great opportunity as I lead a team of 40 people, and since we have a small branch presence in the country, direct banking is the face of the retail bank for the majority of our customers. This is a great challenge and an excellent opportunity to learn a huge amount in a short time.*

SOURCE (HSBC Group, 2012a, b)

In context – forms of employment

Not all employment is full time and permanent. Organizations need to maintain flexibility and they have done this by being able to alter the numbers of employees at one time. They have a core number of employees, specialist staff on permanent contracts and usually full-time. They then have a peripheral set of employees, on atypical contracts such as temporary or fixed-term contracts or part-time permanent contracts. As these peripheral employees tend to be working on less critical tasks it is easier to expand and contract using this set of employees.

The use of the peripheral workforce enables organizations to protect themselves from changes in economic conditions and changing demand for their products or services. It also influences the decision-making of MNCs as they settle on where to establish their production sites. It is very attractive to MNCs and other businesses to have employment laws that give organizations the ability to have a flexible workforce. For example the retail sector needs the ability to take on extra staff to cover the increase in Christmas demand.

Employees, on the other hand, have a need for job security. Some employees wish to have atypical work contracts; often those with caring responsibilities prefer part-time or term-time working and some other employees can accommodate fixed-term contracts, where they take short-term projects and can adjust for times of unemployment. To provide the employer with flexibility some employees are only offered atypical work contracts and have no choice. At the present time in the UK, whilst the level of unemployment has reduced, a large number of newly employed people have had to accept part-time work as it is the only type of work on offer (Kollewe, 2012). There has been a similar effect in Norway which has been addressed by Government intervention – in the State Health Service the Government provides funding to reduce involuntary part-time working (Nergaard, 2011).

In order to protect employees, legislation has been approved to reduce any adverse impact of atypical work. The Agency Workers Regulations 2010 attempts to ensure that temporary employees are not treated less favourably than permanent employees, but this reduces the flexibility that employers have. Similarly, legislation has been passed to support part-time employees – Part-time Workers (Prevention of Less Favourable Treatment) Regulations 2000.

If the law provides security to both parties, without either feeling that they have been compromised, then there is a good basis on which to build the employment relationship.

The employment relationship

Businesses could not survive without their employees, who enable them to provide goods and services to their customers and clients. The relationship through which this is carried out is known as the 'employment relationship'. This can be seen in the formal employment contract, the communication between the organization and the employee, and the systems and rules that enforce the relationship. There are three ways the employment relationship can be viewed and these are in terms of an economic, legal or social perspective.

The economic perspective

Social Exchange Theory (Blau, 1964) views the employment relationship as a transaction, where the true worth of the relationship is assessed by balancing the costs against the benefits. This can be applied to the work context by reviewing the costs of work to the individual (for example effort, time and travel) against the benefits of work (for example, increased satisfaction, self-esteem and payment). The employer also will weigh up the costs against benefits. If the benefits outweigh the disadvantages the employee will remain within the relationship with the employer or vice versa. However, if the cost is too high the employee (or employer) will abandon the relationship and respectively resign or dismiss.

In this economic transaction the employee is the owner of their product (work) which they sell for a price (wage). A free market economy based on supply and demand means that those with scarce skills may be able to obtain the highest wage and conversely those with the more readily available skills can only achieve a low wage. In this free market, the employment relationship can be perceived as purely economic in nature, with competition setting the 'price' of work or wage. This is similar to the approach taken by Adams' Market Exchange Theory (1776) where the market assesses the value of a commodity, in this case, work. However, this free market view of the employment relationship does not take into account that the power, and therefore the ensuing relationship between the organization and the employee, is not equal.

Another view of this economic transactional approach to the employment relationship is the work–wage bargain (Behrend, 1988). The employment contract controls the work–wage bargain, establishing terms of payment for work, but not the specifics about what particular work is to be provided or how. Therefore this does not accurately describe the economic transaction of the employment relationship, as the employee does not just offer work but can make varying degrees of effort. Behrend describes the effort–work bargain and the effort that an employee contributes as lying between '*the highest level which an employee can reach and the lowest one which an employer will tolerate*' (Behrend, 1988: 53). We need to get the best quality and quantity of work from an employee without exploiting them, recognizing that we represent the employer, the stronger of the two parties but also we have a long-term responsibility to protect the employer's reputation.

Viewing the employment relationship as an economic transaction enables us to understand some of the motivations and needs of both parties, but it does not provide all the answers. It fails to account for those employees who make an additional effort outside of their purely contractual obligations, as may be seen for example in the Charitable Sector or in the Healthcare Sector. Also a solely economic relationship implies that employers are interested in profit alone, or worse that they would exploit for profit.

The legal perspective

As many intervening mechanisms for regaining balance in the employment relationship are legal in nature, it is appropriate now to review the legal perspective. According to the International Labour Organisation '*the employment relationship is a legal notion widely used in countries around the world to refer to the relationship between a person called an "employee" (frequently referred to as "a worker") and an "employer" for whom the "employee" performs work under certain conditions in return for remuneration*' (ILO, 2006: 3). Each party in the employment relationship has both rights and responsibilities that have a legal basis and the employment contract, whether written or oral, provides a formal and legal record of the agreements. The employment relationship only includes those with an employment contract (a contract of service), and excludes those workers such as the self-employed, who have a contract for services.

However an employment contract is in place, employees with varying types of contracts, for example part-time or fixed term, are viewed by the law as still having an employment relationship. The contract is unambiguous to both parties, or if not can be clarified by discussion and rewriting and the obligations contained in the contract can be remedied if the written contract is broken, because these obligations are explicit. Employees have some remedy for obligations that are unwritten and implied. These implied duties include the duty of mutual trust and confidence and the employee may, in certain circumstances, obtain this by resigning and claiming constructive dismissal.

The social perspective

The employment relationship also has a social perspective, (Sisson and Storey, 2000). Employees may work alone, but it is more common that employees work as part of a team – The WERS 2004 survey gives the percentage of employees working as part of a team as 72 per cent (Kersley *et al*, 2005: 20). In matrix organizations, where there are many different projects in which employees participate, employees may be part of many different teams. Global working has also developed the use of virtual team-working, with modern fibre optic technology supporting rapid worldwide communications. This close proximity to a range of different employees makes collective bargaining possible and provides the environment for norms to become established clarifying acceptable behaviour in the employment relationship.

The employment relationship is a key concept in Employee Relations. In practice we may focus on the economic and legal aspects of the employment relationship. This leads to a transactional relationship in which terms and conditions are enforced. To overlook the social aspect of the employment relationship is to overlook the effect of employee interactions at work, whether they are to moderate or intensify expectations of employees. It also overlooks the other motivational factors that influence employee engagement and contribute to an individual's higher productivity, lower absence and retention in the organization. The following case studies take a look at the employment relationship within a challenging economic environment.

CASE STUDY   The employment relationship in the UK

Whilst the UK is no longer (in 2013) in the very deep recession of 2008 it is unlikely that many would be able to state that the UK has recovered. The signs of growth have been very weak, stunted but resilient in such difficult times. What has been an interesting phenomenon is unemployment. This has not been as high as in other times of economic hardship, though it remains challenging to find a job.

The Recruitment and Employment Confederation CEO Kevin Green said: '*More people in work than ever before and the lowest unemployment in over a year is another significant step on the road to recovery. The truly amazing thing is that during the past year of a technical recession and in spite of austerity and public sector cuts, the UK has created half a million jobs*' (REC, 2012). Yet according to the Low Pay Commission Report (2013) many new jobs have been within the low paid sector.

'*The job numbers are being driven by flexible working – the number of full-time posts has grown but the increase in temps and part-time workers has been even greater. Too many people talk down the value of part-time work, but it's here in black and white – over 80 per cent of part-time employees chose to work that way*' (REC, 2012). Whilst many have chosen to take temporary and part-time work many are unable to find a full-time job and have decided that a part-time or temporary job is better than no job at all.

A clear picture is given by the Low Pay Commission (2013: 36) which states that:

> *between May 2008 and October 2012, the number of permanent employees fell by 585,000 (2.4 per cent), while the number of temporary employees increased by 14.1 per cent. The number of temporary workers had fallen more or less continuously from 1.79 million in December 1997 to 1.36 million in October 2008. However, during the economic downturn, employers made increasing use of temporary workers and their numbers picked up to reach 1.63 million in July 2012. The increase in those who would have preferred a permanent job (0.31 million) was greater than the total increase in temporary jobs (0.27 million).*

Many people have chosen part-time jobs so they can manage other caring commitments, for example, and employees with a range of commitments, including study or between permanent jobs, may choose temporary assignments. However, for many of these employees the economic perspective has the prerogative, with the need to build longstanding relationships at work much less important when the need to support the family and its financial commitments are the priority.

CASE STUDY   Deregulation policies

As a response to recession, governments around the world have taken mea-sures to improve economic growth, reduce fiscal deficit and unemployment (McDermott and Westcott, 1996). There are few options available for govern-ments with a fiscal deficit – for example, they may invest in public infrastructure, stimulating job creation in associated businesses, but to fund this requires an increase of that debt. One of the approaches taken to stimulate job creation has been to moderate legislation so that employment is less of a risk for employers.

The logic surrounding this is that, by reducing protection, employers' ability to manage the supply of employees is easier. By increasing probation periods and reducing notice periods and redundancy pay, employers can manage the supply of employees both effectively and efficiently. Some countries have gone so far as to reduce employment protection for not just full-term permanent employ-ment but also fixed-term and temporary contracts. Examples range across all income grouped countries (those with high, medium and low national incomes). For example, in Hungary the remedy for unfair dismissal has changed from an uncapped amount to 12 months' salary; and in Portugal redundancy pay has reduced from 30 days to 20 days (for contracts after 1 November 2011) (ILO, 2012a).

The psychological contract

Whilst the written legal contract makes clear the obligations and rights of both parties in the employment relationship, it does not fully describe that relationship. Psychological contracts are the beliefs that people hold about the terms and conditions of their employment relationships (Rousseau, 1989). They are implied rather than written down and are based on the perceptions of both parties about their obligations. And yet, even being just implied rather than expressed they are no less important as they may be the reasons why an employee leaves and we as HR professionals need to find a replacement.

Rousseau (1989) goes on to review two types of psychological contract. The transactional psychological contract, also described by MacNeil (1974,

1985), is short-term and self-interested, with little loyalty or commitment given by either side. For example, the employee is not committed to work long hours but may do so if they are paid highly. The alternative is the relational psychological contract, which is long-term, with strong commitment and loyalty from employees. From an employer's perspective, organizations would like to have in its key roles fully engaged employees with a strong relational psychological contract.

It is thought that the psychological contract has changed dramatically as job security has become less available in modern working life; many employers nowadays find it difficult to offer job security. From the employees' perspective loyalty (as seen in employment tenure) remains strong (People Management, 2003), but employees are committed to their team first and there is weaker commitment to their organization (CIPD, 2012a).

The psychological contract is pivotal to Employee Relations and this is particularly true if it is broken, when we as HR professionals have to manage grievance proceedings. Though the psychological contract can be broken by either party, it is more relevant in Employee Relations to look at the violation of the employee's contract. Rousseau (1995) suggests three situations in which the psychological contract may be broken:

- when the employee's psychological contract may have been broken unintentionally by the employer through misunderstanding;
- when the employer is unable to meet their obligations; or
- when they are unwilling to meet their obligations.

What is important is the perception of the reasons for the breach and research by Dulac *et al* (2008) takes this further. In the event of a breach, the employee will experience emotional distress, may lose both trust and commitment to the employer and may even choose to leave the organization. However, where employees have prior experience of support and the relationship with the Line Manager is good, employees will experience less negative response. This is particularly important as employees experiencing breach may lose trust but they are less likely to leave.

Without trust in the employer the employment relationship becomes transactional, focussed on self-interest and likely to be short-term. Employees are not committed to the organization and need to be rewarded or coerced. Then we, as HR professionals, spend more time devising reward mechanisms to pay employees to give their best, something they might have given with commitment to the organization without complicated and expensive pay systems.

An understanding of the psychological contract is important for anyone managing the employment relationship or dealing with employee disputes and grievances. Some employee grievances have a depth of feeling that may be difficult for those dealing with the grievance to understand. For example, removal of staff discounts in a school canteen or other preferential treatment refer to their status and value and is part of the psychological contract, far outweighing any possible financial loss.

The role of power and authority in the employment relationship

Power is the capacity to direct the behaviours and decisions of others and it is what managers require to meet their objectives. Authority is *'the right to give orders and the power to exact compliance'* (McKenna, 2006: 461). Power is particularly important with organizations that accept that different groups and individuals will have different interests, needs and motives. For example, you as an HR professional may be interested in developing their skills in managing grievance and discipline, where your employer already has someone with this skill but needs someone to cover recruitment and selection. Another instance may be when an employee may wish to work at one location, with one particular Line Manager, as it is near their home and the Line Manager has low demands on the employee. However, the organization may need the employee to change the place they work and work for a more demanding Line Manager.

Employers have the power to make their employees complete their tasks, but it should not be through coercion. Power through threat of punishment gains only short-term compliance. There are other types of power that a manager can use (Raven and French, 1959). Managers have legitimate power due to their position and they can also use reward. Experts, not just managers, have power to influence others through their knowledge, skills and expertise. For example, in the pharmaceutical and technology industries expertise is particularly highly recognized and employees may be responsible for their own group of clients.

Each person has their own interests at heart. They may be motivated to achieve the organization's goals but also want to have their own needs and interests met. To do this they use a range of techniques – this is known as internal politics. When they have a position of authority and their objectives match those of the organization they may be able to use legitimate power. However, at times managers and employees use political methods to meet their interests. Political behaviour, the use of underhand methods to meet personal needs, is more apparent when resources are scarce or under threat (Ferris and Kacmar, 1992) or there is a low trust culture (McKenna, 2006).

Power, authority and internal politics are very relevant to managers and HR professionals. The misuse of power and the abuse or disrespect of authority is at the root of many discipline and grievance issues and the use of political behaviour can disrupt any plan. It is helpful to recognize the gatekeepers to resources and knowledge who have the key power positions. By recognizing that political behaviour may be more prevalent in times of uncertainty, we can ensure that communication is clear, relevant and comprehensive.

The key contributors to employee relations

Employees and employers are not the only contributors in the employee relationship. Both parties have representation or/and advice from particular agencies, be they a Trade Union or Employer Association. There are also national, European and international bodies that influence the employment relationship. Their role in employee relations will be briefly reviewed.

Trade Unions

The role of Trade Unions is to define, promote and represent the interests of its members, in particular through collective bargaining. According to Unite, the largest Union in the UK, it seeks to fight for equality in the workplace, to advance the interests of employees both in the workplace and politically, and to promote a fair society (Unite, 2008). In the UK the Donovan Commission (*Royal Commission on Trade Unions and Employer's Associations 1965–1968*, 1968) identified the legitimate functions of Trade Unions. These included collectively bargaining over terms and conditions, representing individual employees at grievances or disputes, lobbying (on a range of social and political issues) and influencing Government policy.

The right to associate (to join a Trade Union) and to collectively bargain is voiced in conventions C87 and C98 of the International Labour Organization (ILO, 2012b). These two conventions are core to the ILO and have been ratified by 151 countries and 161 countries respectively. This means that these countries endorse the conventions, recognizing both the right to associate as a member of a Trade Union, and to use that Union to collectively bargain. Some of the few countries that have not ratified these conventions include China and Saudi Arabia, the USA and Iran (ILO, 2012c).

This means that Trade Unions can legally exist across a range of countries and it is as a result of a broad acceptance that employees have interests that need collective representation (Gumbrell-McCormick and Hyman, 2006). This may seem inconsistent with the decline in Trade Unions but collective representation may not always be through a Trade Union. For example, in Germany, where the concept of 'social dialogue' has resonance, there is a dual system of representation with the use of industry-based Trade Unions and Works Councils.

In the UK Unions can be occupationally-based (such as the Royal College of Nursing or National Union of Teachers) or more commonly general and open to all (such as Unite). Each Trade Union consists of its members, who pay a subscription, and a Union representative, who is elected by the membership to represent them to management. The national structure of a Trade Union consists of a national headquarters, with a General Secretary and Executive Committee, and Regional or/and local offices.

Employers' Associations

In the UK, individual employers are represented by Trade or Employer Associations. An example of this is the Engineering Employers Association (EEA), which is the Employers' Association for manufacturing. Its role is to lobby both nationally and internationally on behalf of manufacturing companies. It provides legal advice and support, along with training and publications, both reporting on critical issues affecting the manufacturing industry and guidance on best practice. An HR professional in an engineering company may contact the EEA for up-to-date advice on employment law; it provides twice-yearly employment briefings and advice for strategic decisions on Trade Unions. Whilst Employers' Associations have a role in other countries, their roles may differ. For example, in Germany they have a more active role in collective bargaining.

UK National Bodies

There are both employer and employee representative bodies, along with other agencies, that influence the communication between both parties.

The Confederation of British Industry

The main role of the Confederation of British Industry (CBI) is to represent business and industry at a national and international level and it has a powerful lobbying and campaigning role. It represents over 240,000 businesses of all sizes, and its membership also includes a number of Employer Associations (CBI, 2012). The CBI carries out economic surveys and reports on business-related issues to keep its membership updated on the key concerns.

The Trade Union Congress

The Trade Union Congress (TUC) is the UK federation of Trade Unions. It provides training for Union representatives and attempts to manage any clashes between Unions. It represents the majority of Trade Unions and lobbies Government to support working people and campaigns on those economic and social issues that affect its membership. Internationally, it represents UK employees within the European Union and beyond. Finally, it carries out research on employment-related issues.

The Central Arbitration Committee (CAC)

Whilst an employee can be a member of a Union, the Union can only represent employees collectively to a particular employer if it is recognized by that employer. Union recognition is the process by which a Union establishes that it can collectively bargain for its members.

The Central Arbitration Committee is an independent tribunal which works towards the resolution of collective disputes concerning representation. Whilst employers can voluntarily recognize Unions, if there is a dispute concerning the recognition of a Union for collective bargaining or the bargaining unit, the CAC may be asked to adjudicate. It also has jurisdiction over the release of information concerning collective bargaining.

The Certification Officer

The Certification Officer is responsible for ensuring that Trade Unions (and Employer Associations) are compliant with statutory requirements and manage their funds appropriately. The Certification Officer has an important role in ensuring that Trade Unions are independent. If a Trade Union member believes that the Trade Union has breached its rules, the member can apply to the Certification Officer to make a decision on the complaint. If the complaint is successful then an enforcement order can be made.

The Advisory Conciliation and Arbitration Service (ACAS)

The Advisory, Conciliation and Arbitration Service (ACAS), was established by the Employment Protection Act 1975 to provide third party dispute resolution services. It is funded by the Department for Business, Innovation and Skills (BIS) but is totally independent of the state. It is governed by an independent Council of 11 members all with extensive experience of Employee Relations, from areas as diverse as Trade Unionism, the CBI, business, education and law. The Council leads the strategy and ensures that ACAS meets its objectives while managing public funds prudently.

The role of ACAS is to provide advice to employers on good Employee Relations practice, to promote good practice through training and through its publications and Code of Practices. It promotes three dispute resolution methods, conciliation, arbitration and mediation. We will be looking in detail at mediation in chapter 5 but here will provide a brief definition of the two other methods.

ACAS provides conciliation for all claims to Employment Tribunals and also conciliates in collective disputes. It is a voluntary process in which ACAS conciliators explore the reasons for the dispute, explain each side's position and negotiate an agreement. Arbitration is when an independent person is asked to have an impartial review of the case and will make a decision which is held to by each party.

European Bodies

There are a range of Bodies involved in the employment relationship and Employee Relations at the European level. These might be representative of employers or Trade Unions or take a specific role in the forming of employment legislation.

Firstly European bodies will be discussed before going on to review the role of international bodies and their influence on Employee Relations.

Employee Representation in Europe

In Europe, employees are represented by the European Trade Union Confederation and occupational Trade Union Federations that provide an occupation-specific viewpoint at the European level.

The European Trade Union Confederation (ETUC) is the voice of Trade Unions within Europe. Whilst its membership includes national Trade Union confederations, such as the TUC, it also includes European occupational Trade Union federations, such as the European Confederation of Police (EUROCOP) and the European Confederation of Public Sector Unions (EPSU). The ETUC has an important role in influencing European policy and legislation, through its work with the EU Council, Commission and Parliament. It also has encouraged dialogue with employers at a European level, through relations with other European bodies such as CEEP, UEAPME and Business Europe (ETUC, 2011).

Employers' Representation in Europe

Business Europe is the main representative body for businesses and industry in Europe and it represents business interests to the European institutes with the aim of ensuring corporate competitiveness (Business Europe, 2012). Its membership consists of the Business Federations of European countries, such as the CBI.

The European Association of Craft and Small to Medium-sized Enterprises (UEAPME) represents the interests of smaller organizations. It monitors European policy and legislation and represents its members' interests to the EU institutions (UEAPME, 2012).

The European Centre of Employers and Enterprises providing Public Services (CEEP) represents Public Sector employers and as such its members are from a diverse range of industries from transport, to education and health. Along with Business Europe and the ETUC it is recognized as part of the European Social Dialogue, by which it can influence the development of new European legislation and policy.

Key International Bodies

With the increase of globalization, we often find ourselves responsible for the HR issues of employees in different countries. Multinational corporations may have sites in different countries: for example Apple Inc. has its headquarters in California, in the United States, with subsidiaries in Luxembourg, Ireland, the Netherlands and the British Virgin Islands, and IBM has 14 research and development sites worldwide. Whilst it is outside the scope of this book to review the national Employee Relations systems and Trade Union workings for individual countries, an understanding of the influence of international bodies will support such professionals.

The International Labour Organization

The International Labour Organization (ILO) was established in 1919 and is responsible for introducing labour standards. These standards are then ratified by its member countries, which means that they agree to incorporate them into law, with the help of the ILO if necessary. It supports both Trade Union and employer organizations in different countries, so promoting dialogue between employees and employers.

Global Union Federations

There are eleven Global Union Federations, and these are occupationally based: for example, the International Transport Workers Federation (ITF). Global Union Federations represent the national Unions within that sector. They have an active role in supporting national Unions, as the following case study shows.

CASE STUDY   Union pressure wins removal of strike ban
25 October 2012

Turkey's government has withdrawn a ban on strikes in the country's civil aviation sector following an international campaign led by the ITF and Turkish aviation Union Hava-Is.

The aviation strike ban was added to Law 2822, passed earlier this year. This is now being replaced by a new Collective Labour Relations Law, which is awaiting presidential approval. Although the new law falls seriously short of international standards in relation to Trade Union rights the amendment that took away aviation workers' right to withdraw their labour has been completely removed.

ITF general secretary David Cockroft commented:

This ugly attack on fundamental rights was rightly decried by Turkish aviation Union Hava-Is and by the ITF. We are delighted that those protests have paid off and this shabby piece of legislation has been buried. This fulfils the promise made personally to me by the Turkish labour minister that this provision would be dropped. However, we are still awaiting the results of his promise to intervene to get 305 workers at Turkish Airlines – who were sacked for protesting against the proposed change to the law – reinstated.

ITF president Paddy Crumlin added: 'The ITF and its affiliated Unions shone an international spotlight on Turkey over this ban, and the government has rightly decided that it has to be cancelled. The new law bows to international opinion on the ban, but it fails to address fundamental Trade Union rights, and its provisions potentially breach ILO standards and European Union norms.'

Furthermore, 'It is well past time for Turkish Airlines to put back to work the 305 people who rightly resisted the same legislation that has now been dropped like a hot potato.'

Commenting on the Collective Labour Relations law ITUC general secretary Sharan Burrow said: 'Although we have seen some progress, this bill is still very far from complying with international labour standards.' (International Transport Workers Federation, 2012)

International Trade Union Confederation (ITUC)

The International Trade Union Confederation (ITUC) is the main international Trade Union association representing working people. It works closely on policy developments with the ILO and the United Nations. It takes a broad view of social and labour issues, for example campaigning on child labour and discrimination. It also recognizes the role of global competition and MNCs in weakening the response of Trade Unions at a national level (ITUC, 2006).

The contribution of some these national, European and international bodies is to support the different parties in the employment relationship, supporting and promoting the particular party they represent to policy makers. Others bodies provide advice and support to both parties or support Governments to make appropriate legislation, with the aim of protecting any vulnerable party, to reduce conflict and to ensure the smooth running of the employment relationship.

Involvement and participation

We, as HR professionals and Line Managers, need to use our skills to engage employees and support the employment relationship. Practices that involve employees and provide information that enables them to participate in decision-making will help us create a more engaged workforce.

Involvement

Employee involvement describes a wide range of practices for '*informing and consulting employees about, or associating them with, one or more aspects of running an organisation*' (Gennard and Judge, 2010). Involvement practices aim to produce a committed and informed workforce, which identifies with the goals of the organization and is well-equipped to face the rapid pace of change. Its core methods are communication and consultation.

Communication is the activity of passing information, and employers pass information down to employees using a range of techniques (Table 1.1).

Employers communicate downward to employees to pass on instructions, inform employees about rules and policies, to make announcements or

TABLE 1.1 Techniques for downward communication, adapted from ACAS (2009b) Employee Communications and Consultation

Indirect, written methods	Direct, face-to-face methods	Electronic methods
Company handbooks	Team briefing	Company blogs
Employee information notes	Staff meetings	Company video
In-house journals	Cascade networks	
In-house bulletins	Interdepartmental meetings	
Notice boards	Large-scale meetings	
Letters	Management by walking around	

explain plans. Without timely formal communication from the employer, gossip and rumour fills the gap with misinformation and conjecture. These are destructive as they waste time and often build on fear and uncertainty. In such a working environment it is difficult to foster trust or engage staff.

Information can be passed upwards during appraisal meetings, and through satisfaction surveys or suggestion schemes. Upward communication is vital to a modern organization which needs employees to notify them of potential problems and issues to solve. They need employees to provide innovative ideas and solutions to problems, and finally they need employees' involvement in decision-making. However, this is the area which organizations find the hardest to manage. The effectiveness of upward communication depends on the state of the employment relationship and whether trust exists sufficiently for employees to risk becoming involved.

To cover involvement completely, it is necessary to finish by mentioning consultation. This has a foundation both in the Information and Consultation of Employees Regulations 2004, and the Trade Union and Labour Relations (Consolidation) Act 1992. Consultation is the discussion with employees or their representatives about issues that concern them, in order to seek agreement. Consultation does not require the employer to take the views or opinions of employees into account. However, an exchange of views must take place and it must be carried out in good faith.

Participation

Participation is made up of a range of methods '*which enable and at times empower employees, directly or indirectly, to contribute to the decision-making of the firm*' (Redman and Wilkinson, 2009: 406). This remains a contemporary approach to participation, despite the emergence of the term 'employee voice'. This is because, whilst voice implies an opportunity to speak, participation allows a more active role for employees. Some definitions restrict participation to state schemes of collective participation (Hyman and Mason, 1995) and there is some academic dispute about terms, but it seems appropriate for the practical use of Human Resource professionals and Line Managers to withdraw themselves from academic disagreement and to choose a definition which helps them to implement participation in their own organizations.

Modern participation is a long way from Taylor's Scientific Management (1911), when it was viewed as contemporary to reduce tasks down to the minimum so that employees became highly skilled at one particular, routine repetitive task. Now there is a better understanding of the motivation of employees, and there is an attempt to link this to increased effectiveness and productivity. The modern employment relationship also provides scope for both collective participation and individual participation.

When looking at the different approaches that could be used to enable employees to participate, Salamon (2000: 373) provides an effective approach, showing that greater employee control, such as European Works Councils (EWC) and Employee Directors, provide greater participation (see Figure 1.1).

Whilst individual methods will be discussed later, it is important here to take a broader view. One of the key aspects that influence the effectiveness of participation schemes is the commitment that is made by the organization to true participation – the presence of a scheme alone is not sufficient (Marchington and Kynighoe, 2012). There is also a trend in the UK towards direct participation rather than representative participation (Kersley *et al*, 2005: 13–14) despite the legislative foundation for the latter in terms of European Works Councils. This may indicate a concern that indirect participation may reduce the responsiveness of organizations, but the Information and Consultation of Employees Regulations (2004) stipulates a legislative framework for collective consultation at the very least.

FIGURE 1.1   Methods of Participation adapted from Salomon (2000)

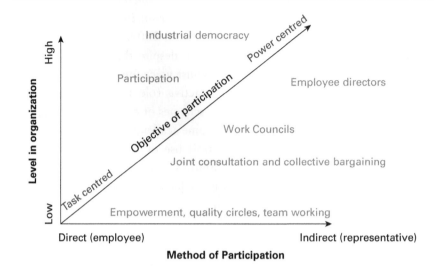

Employee voice

Employee voice is the two-way communication between the employer and the employee. Often communication can seem to be one way, but employee voice is listening and acting on what has been heard so that employees can influence decision-making.

With the decline of Union membership enabling employees to have a voice has increasingly become an issue. With a powerful collective voice employees had a means to be heard and to influence decisions, and also they had the security to speak anonymously. But now, increasingly, individual employees need to be able to represent themselves, they need to be fully aware of the issues so that they can act constructively in their comments and discussions.

Society's approach to voice has changed, and it is in general a more assertive and able workforce that now represents itself. But there are a number of assumptions in this self-reliance. It assumes that:

- the individual employee has the power and influence to make their own voice heard without any further implications for their job security;

- management wishes employees to voice opinions; and
- employees can be and wish to be empowered.

It is necessary to define the scope that an individual voice covers. At one extreme the employee may wish to voice a grievance, to articulate dissatisfaction and at the other extreme employees may wish to contribute to management decision-making or be involved in an Employee Forum (Dundon and Gollan, 2007). Therefore, employee voice may include participation or involvement, at one level with a complaint about an issue that directly affects them or at another by contributing to decision-making. It is the ability of employees to communicate their viewpoint, to be heard and to influence decision-making.

At a fundamental level employee voice has a close relationship with procedural justice – the right to procedures of both grievance and appeal. The availability of voice to enable involvement in decision-making can influence employee engagement. Both facets of employee voice are important if employees are to be engaged and productive.

Conflict

Conflict occurs when the different parties perceive a threat to their needs or interests. Conflict is the struggle to ensure their needs or interests are met. Whenever possible the parties attempt to maintain co-operation as their future depends on working together. However, there are times when conflict occurs and this can be a conflict between individuals, an individual and the organization or collective conflict between a group of employees and the organization.

Cooperation in the workplace

Employers and employees unite in the interest of organizational survival and job security. Employees ultimately need to have secure employment and they depend on their employer for this – they need to be sure that they can bring home a regular salary. The employer depends on the employee for their skills and effort in order to keep the organization profitable. Therefore, all things being equal, co-operation achieves the goals of both employer and employee.

Mutuality and fairness

The legal contract defines the mutual obligations of the employer and employee. Mutuality describes the reliance of both parties on each other, an interdependence or partnership. Employees need payment to maintain a standard of living for them and their families, and conversely employers need to produce goods or services. Therefore, there is a mutual interdependence on one another.

Employees expect to be treated fairly; that the treatment is legal, as described in the employment contract and according to employment statute and case law. They do not expect the contract to be broken. They also anticipate that their expectations, as perceived in the psychological contract, will be met by the employer and that the psychological contract will not be violated. If the employees' expectations are not met then those who believe that they have been treated unfairly will often respond by reducing their work performance and their commitment to the organization (Colquitt *et al*, 2001).

Fairness is the perception of being treated equally along with other colleagues. Justice is the right of an individual to what they perceive they are due. For example, an employee may believe that, because of their exceptional skills and knowledge they are due a higher salary than others in the team. However, others may not agree and see this as unfair because payment is unequal.

There are four types of justice that apply to the employment relationship:

- **Distributive justice** is the perceived fairness of the allocation of rewards. The example above, which discusses justice in relation to pay, refers to distributive justice.
- **Procedural justice** relates to the fairness of the procedures used, and employees evaluate the fairness against a number of criteria. These include how the organization selects managers in the process, the method used to collect information, how the decisions are made, and whether there is access to an appeals process (Leventhal, 1980). An employee may perceive a procedure as unfair if there was no ability to appeal a decision.

- **Interactional justice** relates to the relationship the manager has with the employee and fairness within the supervisory relationship. This could include the manager's dishonesty, invasion of an employee's privacy, disrespectful treatment and derogatory judgements (Bies, 2001). An employee may accept a low pay rise if they are given a clear explanation and treated with respect by their Line Manager.

- **Informational justice** refers to the transparency of information about the process. Some employers make sure all procedures are clearly explained on their intranet site.

Stages of conflict

There are three views of conflict – unitarist, pluralist and interactional:

- **Unitarist** views of conflict dictate appropriate employee behaviour: conflict is viewed as disruptive and disloyal and Union activity is opposed.

- **Pluralist** views accept that employees may have different values and divergent goals, with acceptance of the Trade Union role and the need for compromise.

- **Interactionist** views accept conflict as this encourages innovation and helps the organization to respond to change quickly (McKenna, 2006).

However, conflict is not a comfortable state for employees – in fact, conflict has been defined as '*differences in ideas and opinions, which give rise to tension among the group members*' (Ayub and Kahn, 2011). This hints at the first facet of conflict, which is its role in innovation, something that we as HR professionals should encourage. But conflict has many different aspects, and a further definition describes conflict as the process of frustration of an individual's or group's goals by another individual or group (Thomas, 1992). This clearly accounts for the involvement of internal politics in conflict, as do Appelbaum *et al* (1999: 62), who describe conflict as '*a process of social interaction that involves a struggle over claims to resources, power and status, beliefs, preferences and desires*'. This struggle will be familiar to us and is clearly apparent in the working lives of employees and managers. Whether a conflict over operational issues, frustration over the timescale of a project or over budgetary resources, conflict is natural and we should help Line Managers to manage it.

It is in the management of conflict that we may struggle because employees' responses are primitive and can be emotional. It is therefore helpful to determine the different stages that a conflict may go through. Often we only become aware of conflict at the escalation or stalemate stages and they are often involved in supporting employees through to the negotiation stage. Perceptive Line Managers may recognize the latent stage of conflict, when there is, for example, perceived unfairness or lack of resources, and they may intervene to resolve if possible any causes of conflict, or if this is not possible to provide an explanation for the situation.

FIGURE 1.2   Conflict Stages adapted from Brahm (2003)

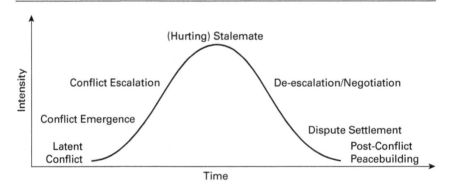

Causes of conflict

To start the process of analyzing the causes of conflict writers have found it necessary to classify the different types of conflict. This is helpful as it assists us to refer back to our experience of conflict. Both ACAS (2009a) and writers such as Jehn and Mannix (2001) have attempted to categorize conflict.

According to ACAS (2009a) conflict can occur between individuals, between groups (intergroup conflict) or within groups (intragroup conflict). When it occurs between individuals it may be between colleagues or between a manager and an employee. Conflict can also be categorized into three different types (Jehn, 1997; Jehn & Mannix, 2001):

- conflicts over task;
- conflict over process; and
- difficult relationships.

This approach starts to analyze cause, which enables us to more effectively support resolution of the conflict. Task conflict is where disagreements occur over the content of the task, over the goals of the project and what needs to be done. Task conflict is natural and the result of people with different views working together – it can be positive as new and innovative ways of working can come about as a result. We don't usually find that these conflicts involve HR unless during this conflict issues over employee relationships become involved. Process conflict is where there are disagreements over the allocation of resources or tasks – for example, if an employee feels that the tasks given to them are too great a burden or that they do not have enough time to complete the tasks effectively. This can cause resentment, as employees may feel that they are being asked to do the impossible. Finally, relationship conflict involves problems with the interactions themselves, where different personalities find it difficult to work together. These can cause difficulty for Line Managers and HR professionals as it can affect the performance of the department and lead eventually to employees leaving.

Mullins (2005) describes a number of causes of conflict, a list that is not exhaustive but includes differences in perception, scarce resources, different goals, interdependence of work, inequitable treatment and individual needs, attitudes or personality. The CIPD identifies causes of conflict with Line Managers, and areas such as absence and drug use, which are unacceptable behaviour by employees enforced by company policy. The CIPD also provide a number of different less apparent sources of conflict, such as '*taking credit for other people's work or ideas, talking over people in meetings and not inviting team members to team social evenings or events*' CIPD (2008). Many of these are relationship conflicts based on a lack of respect and different goals.

Forms of employee conflict and misbehaviour

Employees can act to foster their own interests or can honestly disagree with the employer. This informal action will be unorganized, not supported by a Union and is individually-driven. Such action may include absenteeism, reduced effort, withdrawal of co-operation or sabotage and the results of such action to the company range from minimal to catastrophic. Many organizations are most vulnerable to loss of information, as the case study below shows.

CASE STUDY   Case studies of sabotage

Sabotage as a form of conflict would be thought of as rare and in fact many employees are not in the position to sabotage anything of value to the employer, and if they were may also fear for their own position and any criminal charges that may be made as a result.

It can occur when an employee is being made redundant and feels that there is little to lose. In this case it can be either an act of self-interest, for example when files are taken so that an ex-employee can then use them to build a business with the employer's customers, or an act of revenge. Two examples of revenge, one at Omega Engineering and the other at Walt Disney, show the costs of such action.

> *At Omega Engineering, a computer-systems administrator crashed Omega's companywide server and stole vital backup files. Production ground to a halt. Despite the best efforts of a team of data recovery experts, Omega lost about $10 million and countless files.*
>
> *At Walt Disney, an employee tampered with video release versions of the animated film 'The Rescuers', and embedded an obscene photograph in two frames. Disney responded by recalling 3.4 million videos.*
>
> Forman and Watkins (2009)

More often it can be disgruntled employees who, if for example have been passed over for a promotion, may claim discrimination. These claims may take valuable time as they go through formal internal processes but the disgruntled employee may make costly Employment Tribunal claims which, with legal costs, can be damaging to the company. They may threaten the employer's reputation and lead to the employer choosing to make a financial settlement with the employee rather than face an Employment Tribunal – unfounded claims can cost a company a great deal.

HR professions can protect the company by ensuring that procedures are transparent and decisions recorded, so that there is evidence that employees have not been discriminated against. They can make sure that employees that are at risk of redundancy are treated with respect and consideration so that there are fewer reasons for acts of revenge. Finally they can ensure that processes are put in place to protect the company, including restrictive covenants in employment contracts and removal of IT access when employees leave.

While the results of sabotage can be costly to an organization, it is an extreme and atypical response of an employee. More common forms of dissent are lack of engagement and effort, time wasting and absenteeism. These are also costly to the organization, and such informal disputes need to be resolved.

Collective Conflict

Collective disputes are of a different magnitude and often larger organizations have a disputes procedure in place. Traditionally in the UK collective representation has been through a Trade Union recognized by the employer, with disputes of terms and conditions being negotiated and compromises made. Section 178 of the Trade Union and Labour Relations (Consolidation) Act (1992) identifies the areas that are covered under collective bargaining. Where no agreement is made then there are options to involve third parties to resolve the dispute. After third party resolution efforts have been made, if there is no agreement then a Trade Union may well resort to strike action.

The end of the employment relationship

An employee may choose to end the employment contract by resigning and an employer ends the employment relationship by dismissing the employee. Usually the other party is not ready for the employment relationship to end; it's rare that both parties are equally content to part company.

Dismissal

In the UK the employee, in general, has protection against unfair dismissal after two years' service. There are a number of different steps an employer must take to ensure a dismissal is fair and the first is to ensure that the reason for dismissal is a fair one.

According to section 98 of the Employment Rights Act 1998 there are five reasons that an employer can dismiss an employee and it is important to clarify the reason for dismissal. These reasons are:

- misconduct;
- capability;
- redundancy;

- legal restrictions;
- some other substantial reason.

Substantial misconduct is a common reason for dismissal and an employee will be seen as being dismissed for misconduct if their behaviour or actions have been unacceptable. Misconduct includes lateness or abusive language whilst gross misconduct refers to misconduct which is exceptional and will need to be dealt with severely. Gross misconduct can include actions such as financial fraud, dishonesty, disloyalty, violence or subordination.

There are two distinct strands of capability. One refers to the inability of an employee to meet the required quantity or quality of work through lack of skill, knowledge or aptitude. The second refers to absence from work due to long-term or frequent physical or mental illness. Capacity is an example of the effort–work bargain – if the employer is not able to obtain the expected effort from the employee, then the benefit gained from work is not sufficient and the employee will be dismissed.

Redundancy will be reviewed as a topic alone as it is a complex and common method of dismissal – the last two reasons are less common. Legal restrictions are restrictions on an employee's ability to participate in work. For example, a taxi-driver could be dismissed for a drink-driving ban as driving without a valid licence would contravene the law. 'Some other substantial reason' includes particular business needs and pressure from third parties, but is not a catch-all to enable employers to dismiss without meeting the fair reasons of section 98 of the Employment Rights Act 1996. In practice the first three fair reasons – conduct, capability and redundancy – are the most common.

There are reasons for dismissal which are automatically unfair and for these there is no required length of service. These reasons are extensive but are generally based on protecting the employee from perverse dismissal decisions. Automatically unfair reasons include dismissal as a consequence of (section 98B to 104F of the Employment Rights Act):

- taking jury service;
- refusing to work on a Sunday;
- discrimination due to pregnancy and maternity;
- other discrimination as stated in the Equality Act 2010 – protection against discrimination on the grounds of age, disability, gender

    reassignment, marriage and civil partnership, pregnancy and maternity, race, religion or belief, sex and sexual orientation;

- requesting parental leave, paternity leave (birth and adoption), adoption leave or time off for dependants;

- acting as an employee representative and Trade Union membership;

- seeking flexible working;

- seeking the minimum wage or requesting holiday or rest (Working Time Regulations);

- seeking to claim working tax credits;

- notifying the organization of a health and safety issue;

- making a 'protected disclosure' – notifying the organization or an appropriate person about an illegal or serious wrongdoing;

- being on a prohibited or 'blacklist'.

Employees are entitled to notice. The minimum is one week per years' service for the first two years starting at one month after the contract commences, with a maximum notice of 12 weeks (section 86, Employment Rights Act 1996).

Redundancy

The legal definition of redundancy can be found in section 139 of the Employment Rights Act 1996. The Act describes three circumstances when dismissal due to redundancy occurs. The first is when the redundancy is due to the employer ending its business, for example by going into administration. The second circumstance is when the employer is ending business at that particular site and the third circumstance is when work is either reduced or ceases altogether.

How to carry out a redundancy will be covered later, but at this stage it is necessary to clearly understand what redundancy is. It is the ending of a job or role rather than the dismissal of a person. If the role is unnecessary then the person carrying out the role must leave the organization – a redundancy. This is an important point as it attempts to reduce any rejection an employee may feel over the redundancy. However, the particular circumstances of the redundancy will also influence this. If the employer is insolvent and is either going into liquidation or administration then employees may believe that the role is being ended as the company is dissolved, no longer being a legal and functioning business; if the employee is the only one being made redundant then the interpretation of the situation is very different.

According to ACAS (2012) *'about 150,000 workers in the UK are taking voluntary redundancy or being made redundant every three months – and that trend has been constant for the past 12 months as the nation wrestles against the economy's downturn'*. Redundancy is a common experience for many in the UK.

Conclusion

Whatever stage in the employee cycle we are involved in, and whether we are a Recruitment and Selection Specialist, an HR Administrator, a Business Partner or HR Generalist, when we relate to employees or support Line Managers we are likely to be involved in Employee Relations. An understanding of best practice helps us to manage this effectively. We need to encourage Line Managers to talk with and listen to employees and to involve them by asking for their ideas and suggestions. An understanding of power and the psychological contract, along with conflict, helps us understand why disputes and disagreements occur and how best to resolve these. So our actions influence Employee Relations, for example, when we listen to an employee grievance, prepare a contract or support reward strategies that engage employees.

In this chapter we have had to bring in some theory to explain Employee Relations. In the following chapter we will explain in more detail why an understanding of Employee Relations is important.

CASE STUDY   The role of other civil organizations in Employee Relations

With the reduction of Union membership and the need to support employees who do not have a Trade Union to represent them, the profile of voluntary organizations, such as the Citizens Advice Bureau (CAB) has increased. The

CAB provides widespread support for the community, including advice and information to individuals on benefits and those having problems with managing debt, and caters to a growing demand for employment advice in the community (CAB, 2013). CAB provides advice and support for line managers managing grievance and disciplinary actions and, where necessary, to those making Employment Tribunal claims, on some occasions representing employees.

Then there are voluntary organizations with a more specialist remit. Organizations such as SCOPE and Carers Trust provide support for disabled people and carers, respectively. As the needs of their membership may cover a wide area, both organizations need to provide advice and information on this wide variety of issues. SCOPE has a 'Diversity Works' initiative to encourage employers to employ people with a learning disability and Stonewall has Diversity Champions, both providing support to employers on discrimination.

The role of these voluntary organizations extends beyond the advice they give to employees, and organizations such as Stonewall and Carers Trust may have a lobbying role. Though this is not looking at individual voice, it provides a national voice to Government in terms of their membership.

Heery *et al* (2012) discuss the role of these types of organization as being deemed able to access both legitimate and expert power. These organizations are able to take a moral standpoint, so their argument when lobbying is strengthened. One of their strengths is their ability to work with other organizations in their campaign to improve working conditions. For example:

> *One of our strengths is working in alliances, we have really good relationships with all sorts of quite diverse organizations, because of the nature of home-workers there are lots of different angles; it's a women's issue, it's a low pay issue, it's a poverty issue, it's an employment rights issue, it's an international issue, so we make lots of different connections.*
>
> Abbott *et al* (2012: 96)

In some respects pressure groups and voluntary organizations are filling the gap that Trade Unions once occupied. This does not fully meet the support that Trade Unions provided in the workplace, but society's approach to voice has changed. Whether the balance of power has truly changed towards the employee remains arguable.

The importance of Employee Relations

02

INTRODUCTION

There are very few Employee Relations professionals and experience and skills take time to build. Yet, it is argued in this chapter that Employee Relations is vital to the organization and its future success. In this chapter we will explore:

- the need for Employee Relations and in particular the role that it plays:
  - in ensuring an organization complies with legislation
  - in the perception of an organization as acting ethically
  - in building competitive advantage;
- the role of conflict in innovation;
- how the Employee Relations professional can support conflict management;
- the part played by involvement and participation in employee and company performance.

Employee Relations and the employment relationship

As we have seen in Chapter 1, Employee Relations reflects the relationship between the employer and employee. The employee relationship has economic transactional, legal and social components and both parties in the relationship have rights and needs.

The employer's right to manage

For an organization to function effectively and to meet its overall business strategy a manager must have the right to manage through the authority that they have been given by the status of manager. Whilst throughout the book we stress the value of involving employees, if employees continuously questioned management decisions, and managers were not left to manage, no work would ever get completed. Fayol (1949) described management as having five elements – to forecast and plan, to organize, to command, to co-ordinate and control – and it is clear that management decisions can only be implemented through people. Managers need to direct and co-ordinate behaviour and action for three main reasons:

- to ensure that all happens in accordance with the operational plan;
- to maintain control of costs and manage the efficient use of scarce resources; and
- to provide an environment of order and stability for work to be carried out effectively.

It is in this context, with the need for management control as agreed by both parties, that the employment relationship exists.

The employee's rights protected

Employees enter employment with an understanding that there are factors other than an economic transaction involved; that there are legal obligations that the employer will meet and that their rights will be protected. There are also obligations, often ambiguous and hidden, part of the employee's psychological contract that the employee expects to be met. An employer also understands that an employee expects payment, that any interaction with the employee will be within the law and that there are some obligations that the employee might expect to be met, but these last obligations may not be clear to the employer. So the employment relationship begins with similar expectations of the employee rights, with the employee expecting to be treated both legally and ethically.

At times even the basic employee rights are not protected and the needs of the business unreasonably take precedent. The case study below shows how the decisions of managers put employees' lives at risk. Employers do not meet their obligation to provide employees with a safe working environment when costs cut risk lives.

CASE STUDY   The Deepwater Horizon accident

On 20 April 2010 an explosion on the Deepwater Horizon Oil Rig in the Gulf of Mexico killed 11 employees. The rig burnt for 36 hours before sinking but a more catastrophic result was that for the three months following the accident 4.9 million barrels of crude oil flowed from the rig (Hock, 2012). This caused widespread pollution across the Gulf of Mexico from Louisiana to Florida, damaging wildlife, marine stocks and tourism in the area.

A subsequent report, commissioned by the White House, concluded that the cause of the accident was a series of cost-cutting decisions. Cement was pumped into the well by BP's partner Halliburton, but there was no diagnostic testing by BP to ensure that the cement was adequately stable. BP then relied on the cement as a barrier to the flow of crude oil and gas, and the cement ultimately failed. Transocean, who managed the Deepwater Horizon rig, had experienced a similar incident on a North Sea rig but had not communicated this to those on the Deepwater Horizon rig. (The Telegraph, 2011)

The case study shows that the three companies failed to 'command, co-ordinate and control' and protect employees' rights and safety – BP, Transocean and Halliburton were basically unethical.

The ethical imperative

Ethics is at the core of the good management of people but to a business the ethical argument for Employee Relations and for building a good employment relationship is not a priority. For us just to say that it is the 'right thing to do' is not enough. In the absence of employment law, if organizations were free to make choices without sanction, it is unclear whether those choices would be ethical. Yet we as HR professionals have at times been viewed as the moral compass of the organization and it would be helpful if we had a stronger argument than solely morality but that making the ethical choice would improve profitability.

However, this is not possible – whilst there is a clear association between ethical business and improved financial performance it is not clear what is the determining factor – as acting ethically may not increase profit (Fisher and Lovell, 2009). It is not apparent whether being ethical increases profitability or whether with increased profit a company chooses to become more ethical. The larger the company the more they have to lose if their choices are not ethical, and therefore it could be argued that it may be that reputation increases in importance the larger the organization becomes.

Managing ethically is managing people using a fixed and established set of standards about right and wrong and we need to support Line Managers to be able to do this. Ethics pervades management – through the values of the manager and how these are passed on through their actions, and this is what is seen by employees. If Line Managers manage ethically, supporting the team to work well and encouraging employees to take pride in their work, they will foster trust and loyalty. It will build a good relationship between the Line Manager and employee that will retain employees in the organization and maintain communication so that the main obligations inherent in the psychological contract are reasonably clear.

We are also asked to support Senior Managers and CEOs. An important role for Senior Managers and CEOs is to communicate:

- the mission of the organization;
- the organizational culture;
- the set of values which ensure all employees understand acceptable behaviour;
- the key behaviours which are important to the organization.

The values of the organization are communicated, both explicitly in written statements by the organization, and more implicitly in a range of processes: for example, induction courses, coaching, training, and recognition and reward schemes. For MNCs there may be particular challenges as different cultural values are found in different countries. Decisions have to be made on whether the organization is to run global subsidiaries directly from the headquarters and with the use of expatriates (ethnocentric approach) or by the host country and their nationals (polycentric approach). There are obvious difficulties for MNCs when assessing the appropriateness of dictating certain values to subsidiaries and in the management of expatriate employees with differing values from the host country. Whatever decisions are made concerning communicating acceptable behaviour, ethical integrity is vital to a leadership role, and Senior Managers must lead by example as employees will not follow a leader that lacks ethical integrity (Kanungo and Mendonca, 1996).

We also support employees; employees are stakeholders in their company, their future is tied up in the future of the company and the company has obligations to employees. A pluralist approach recognizes the needs of employees, but not to such an extent that all other considerations, including economic, are excluded (Fisher and Lovell, 2009). This approach accepts the organization as a community in which all stakeholders, including managers and shareholders, have interests that the organization has a duty to consider. Part of the stakeholder approach relates to the 'common good', that distribution of profit should be distributed amongst the community of stakeholders. The responsibilities that an organization has to its employees as stakeholders are also identified and these include:

- avoiding using employees as passive producers;
- promoting respect for employees' rights;
- complying with employment law and acting beyond law if the right is not sufficiently protected;
- favouring active dialogue with employees;
- fostering training and development and in particular to ensure employability;
- fostering initiative, independence, responsibility and creativity;
- providing stability in employment;
- encouraging work–life balance.

Melé (2012)

It is clear that ethical management, in terms of Line Managers, Senior Managers and employees, involves building good Employee Relations and employment relationship. We stand between these roles and so it is now appropriate to discuss the part the HR professional plays in ethical management. Ulrich's model of HR (1997) provides four roles for HR professionals – strategic partner, change agent, administrative expert and employee champion. HR has enthusiastically taken the role of strategic partner and, according to the CIPD (2012b), has moved away from only supporting Line Managers to the broader role of managing people appropriately in order to focus on organizational performance and capability. In this shift towards strategic partner it has become difficult for HR to fulfil the role of employee champion – to act as an advocate for employees and protect their needs. However, this still remains an important HR role and puts HR professionals in a very challenging situation.

Whilst recognizing this tension between the needs of business and individuals it is important to remember that we as HR professionals have a code of professional conduct to follow, in which both ethical behaviour and integrity are stressed. According to this code, HR professionals are to:

- *'establish, maintain and develop business relationships based on confidence, trust and respect'*;
- *'exhibit and defend professional and personal integrity and honesty at all times'*;
- *'advance employment and business practices that promote equality of opportunity, diversity and inclusion and support human rights and dignity'*.

(CIPD, 2012c)

With our understanding of employment law we can be viewed as advising on what action is right, within a legal context, and there may be little thought of the ethical considerations on employees. We have a duty, stated in our code of professional conduct, to take an ethical view and to act with integrity.

The legal imperative

We have less difficulty arguing for the need of the organization to meet legal requirements in terms of the employment relationship and Employee Relations. We have an obvious responsibility to protect the organization from litigation, the costs involved and the damage to its reputation, and in doing so can promote the legal rights of employees. However, over time the law changes and this may affect the extent to which the law can apply to the employment relationship.

The state provides the legislative framework for Employee Relations and the approach changes dependent on the Government in power, particular social values and economic circumstances. Farnham (2000: 117) explains that the impact of the law on Employee Relations depends on whether the law:

- focuses on legal rights or legal freedoms of parties;
- is 'abstentionist, interventionist or restrictive';
- prioritizes individual or collective patterns of Employee Relations;
- affects the balance of power between employee and employer.

In the UK employment law has in the past been limited, with the Government preferring not to intervene by making law to ensure fairness, but depending more on the relationship of employer and employee and the fact that they are reliant on each other – this is known as taking a voluntarist approach. However, since the 1970s national, and latterly EU-led, law has influenced the employment relationship, both at collective and individual levels. Employment law continues to be resisted by employers, who prefer a lighter touch. The CBI (2011: 2–3) suggests that 'instead of regulating at every turn, government should set out more of its objectives though flexible means ... and leave it to employers and employees to manage the minutiae of what happens in the workplace'. An alternative view is taken by the TUC (2011). The TUC supports employment law and its impact on the employment relationship because it provides protection for employees.

Employment law has developed to support employee rights and protection. Examples of these rights and protections relating specifically to the employment relationship are given below. The rights and protections of employees are not limited to these examples, but these give a flavour of the extent of and changes to employment legislation. Employees have a right:

- to at least minimum pay rates (National Minimum Wage Act 1998 and Regulations made regularly to amend the rate);
- to maternity pay if eligible (Social Security Act 1986, Statutory Maternity Pay Regulations 1986 and amended regularly to amend the rate);
- to maternity leave if eligible (Employment Rights Act 1996, Employment Relations Act 1999, Maternity and Parental Leave Regulations 1999);
- to request flexible working if eligible (Employment Act 2002, Work and Families Act 2006);

- not to be discriminated against (Equality Act 2010);
- not to be unfairly dismissed (Employment Rights Act 1996);
- to notice of dismissal and redundancy pay if eligible (Employment Rights Act 1996).

The fact that the law on Employee Relations changes with time impacts on HR professionals in two ways. We need to keep up-to-date with changes in legislation, and when responsible for employees in other countries we need to ensure that we have a reliable reference for employment law in the countries employees are based in. Secondly, we still need to rely on an ethical compass, to ensure that good practice is maintained whether the legal approach is abstentionist (limited and allowing more voluntarist approaches), interventionist (intervening to rebalance power), or restrictive (preventing action by employer or employee).

In the case study below we look at how illegal practices can infiltrate an organization to such a degree that they are rarely questioned and become part of the culture. Along with this we also look at how HR professions dealt with the issue. Though there is only limited information we can review how we would have acted in a similar situation.

CASE STUDY   Phone hacking and the News of the World

Phone hacking (the listening to calls and recorded messages of members of the public) was a common but illegal practice carried out by journalists at The News of the World. When Clive Goodman, the royal editor, was arrested and convicted of the illegal practice, he was dismissed for gross misconduct but received a payment of £90,502 in recognition of his long service. Clive Goodman argued at his appeal that the practice of phone hacking was widespread and known about by management. At this point News International's HR Director, Daniel Cloke, took six weeks to review numerous emails and interviewed colleagues to determine whether there was such widespread practice. Emails were also passed to News International's solicitors, Harbottle & Lewis, for an independent review. No evidence of knowledge of the practice was found.

Whilst this process of investigation was good employment practice the payment of £90,502 in April 2007, and then a further payment of £153,000 between October and December 2007, is more questionable. It is interesting to note that a case of unfair dismissal at an Employment Tribunal would yield a maximum of £60,000 compensation.

Whilst this case study provides the background to the unethical and illegal practices at The News of the World, it is also relevant to question the effect these practices must have had on journalists who had different values to their peers. The implicit acceptance of this practice by management promoted the values of The News of the World.

Adapted from: The House of Commons Culture Media and Sport Committee (2012)

Competitive advantage and employer of choice

To be profitable an organization needs to be as competitive as possible to make money. How an organization does this will depend on the business strategy chosen, but for all employers competitive edge comes through the effective use of its resources, and employees are a key, if not the key, resource. An example of this can be found in the Hospitality Sector, where people are critical to the design and delivery of the service (Mullins, 2001) and therefore the link between employee performance and competitive edge is more obvious. In restaurants and hotels, people provide the service and it is their contribution which can make the difference between a poor and good customer experience. In key departments within an organization, for example in sales or customer services, it is clear that the performance of employees directly influences product and services sold or the satisfaction, and therefore purchasing behaviour of customers.

This is not to say that people provide the only contribution to competitive edge – for example poor facilities at a hotel will reduce customer satisfaction – but the contribution of people is significant. It is recognized in the mission and value statements of organizations such as Coca-Cola, the drinks manufacturer (Coco-Cola, 2010) and Ocado, the online grocery delivery service (Ocado, 2012). Therefore it can be seen that Employee Relations and the employment relationship are of high importance if organizations are to maximize competitiveness through people.

To be competitive organizations need to build a reputation that attracts potential employees and a relationship with the employees that retains them. If the employment relationship is viewed solely from the economic perspective, then to attract employees organizations only need to provide the right pay and benefits. If it meets legal requirements and employees' rights are protected, then potential employees will apply for roles in the organization because they know that their rights will be secure. It is clear that taking either of these perspectives is not adequate when determining what attracts talented potential employees. An organization needs to become an 'Employer of Choice', an organization which candidates will choose as an alternative to other employers. It is the reputation of the organization that attracts potential employees; whether it values its employees enough to reward them suitably, whether work is challenging and there is opportunity for career development, whether the organization behaves ethically in the way it treats its employees (Herman, Gioia and Chalkley, 1998).

Existing employees must also perceive the organization as the 'Employer of Choice'. An organization makes a high investment in its employees, and this includes the costs of recruitment and training. Once fully trained employees contribute to the team any resignation disrupts the effectiveness and efficiency of the work. Whilst some turnover of staff may be planned, it is the unplanned resignation that is costly to an organization, and though employees can choose to leave for many reasons that an employer cannot influence, it is of value to retain employees by reducing the amount of staff turnover. Employees may choose to leave an organization because competition attracts them away by providing improved pay or promotion prospects (pull factors). Employees also leave because they are not satisfied where they are, often because of their relationship with their Line Manager or the inability to meet a request for flexible working (push factors). The fact that an employee leaves in these circumstances indicates that there is serious trouble with the employment relationship. By ensuring that employees have an opportunity to voice dissatisfaction, for example through grievance procedures and EIP methods, any dissatisfaction can be identified and dealt with before an employee resigns. This has been evidenced by Spencer (1986), who showed that the higher the number of mechanisms for employee voice available in an organization the greater the retention rate. This is not to argue that the state of the employment relationship is the key factor determining turnover, but that it plays a significant role.

Employee Involvement and Participation (EIP)

In chapter one the difference between involvement and participation was discussed. Involvement covered the communication and consultation of employees whilst participation was a range of methods instigated by management to encourage or improve decision-making.

EIP and employee performance

The terms employee involvement (which really means communication and consultation) and employee participation (which really means encouraging contribution to decision-making) are combined into one term – Employee Involvement and Participation (EIP). It is not a practical issue but as you read about the subject it may help to see the difference. However we will generally look at employee involvement and participation together and how they may influence an employee's performance in their job.

An employee may be perceived to be performing well if they meet or exceed the standard of work expected of them, in terms of both the quality and quantity of work. They must also do this in a manner consistent with the organization's expectations of behaviour. To perform well an employee must firstly be present at work, have knowledge of work standards and finally must understand values and behaviours that are important to the organization.

How an employee performs in a job will depend on their knowledge, skills and experience and with additional training an employee's performance may improve, not only by the development of skills but by communication of the expected standard of work. Employees cannot meet their performance standards if these are not effectively communicated. The communication of work standards is the responsibility of the Line Manager; good management cannot be carried out without effective communication. The Line Manager will communicate expectations informally through opportunities to discuss expected standards with the individual, and more formally during induction, supervision sessions and appraisals. There are other factors involved in the role of communication and work performance. If employees are satisfied with the extent and quality of communication, employees' absentee rates reduce (Dasgupta, Suar and Singh, 2013) and with better attendance employees have the opportunity to improve their skills and to show that they can perform well. However, performance in a role is also dependent on communication of the organization's values and expectation of behaviour, a role often taken by, but not exclusive to, Senior Managers.

Most employees work as part of a team and communication helps to coordinate teamwork. Communication is also required to plan, to allocate tasks and to monitor progress. Organizations also attempt to communicate and exploit knowledge to gain a competitive advantage. Highly skilled and experienced employees pass on their expertise to the less experienced. Employees may be asked to report back on conferences or training they have undertaken or apply and record knowledge by preparing reports. But, more commonly, knowledge is passed on in the discussions of problems and issues in the routine exchanges of daily work. Managing and using knowledge can be quite simple but are very valuable, as these examples show. As part of an outsourcing and redundancy programme British Gas sent volunteers from the UK to India to train employees on a computerized billing system (Personnel Today, 2005). ABB, an engineering company, established communities of practice between service engineers who carried out maintenance work. In discussions about their client visits, engineers had improved report gathering (People Management, 2011). In both these examples there is clear value added to the performance of the individuals and the team, and also ultimately the organization and customers.

When it comes to participation and employee performance evidence does not show a close link between participation and individual performance. This is because there are so many other factors that influence employee performance, including training and experience.

EIP and organizational performance

Involvement

It is obvious that an organization cannot perform to its full potential if communication to its employees is poor. An organization that also does not listen to its employees will not be informed of areas where improvements can be made. However there is a further part that communication plays. There is a positive relationship between satisfaction with communication and commitment to the organization (Varona, 1996, 2002), and committed employees remain with the organization and work hard.

Participation

There is conflicting evidence of a link between employee participation and organizational performance. Some academics are convinced of the link (Handel and Levine, 2004) whilst others are less confident of this and associate any improvement to organizational performance to a range of factors (Bryson, Forth and Kirby, 2005). In this section we will review the link of participation methods to organizational performance by introducing one particular method – semi-autonomous teams.

Semi-autonomous teams are self-managed working groups where employees have increased discretion and autonomy. They are one form of high involvement practice (such as quality circles). They exist alongside other HR practices and reward processes, such as appraisals and skill-based pay, which together support the motivation and functioning of the team. This together has become known as High Performance Work Practices (HPWP). A package of a bundle of HR practices and semi-autonomous teams have been shown in studies to have a positive impact on organizational performance, (Den Hartog and Verburg, 2004). It is difficult to determine whether this positive impact is as a result of the HR bundles and the participative process itself. Also it may be argued by HPWP employees that any improvement of organizational performance may be as a result of work intensification and not increased commitment.

As mentioned, the academics hold different views on the affect of participation on organizational performance. In many ways it could be argued that employee participation measures play a greater role in engagement, voice and commitment than it does in influencing organizational performance. As such it reduces employee retention and associated recruitment costs and communicates knowledge to improve team performance. The effects of EIP methods also extend further than the organization – it indicates the values of the organization and may promote the brand and its reputation to customers and the community at large.

Finally, to take a European perspective, we may look at social dialogue in the EU. Participation and involvement is an integral part of the European Social Model, with what is termed 'social dialogue' (employee voice) being required to moderate the employment relationship and, where effective, improve productivity. Bryson, Forth and George (2012) carried out research into the different types of social dialogue in Europe, and proposed that the variations in types of employee voice and participation across Europe are the result of cultural and historical reasons rather than any perceived effect on organizational performance in different countries. They also suggested that dialogue may not improve Employee Relations – in fact, good employee voice may result in increased grievance and disharmony. Employee voice can influence the company to increase wages and improve job security, but neither improves organizational performance, and in fact higher wages may reduce profitability. It may be argued that any improvement to organizational performance is a by-product of improved engagement, motivation and the organization's reputation.

The legal imperative

The communication and consultation of employees is enforced by law. The law covers both ongoing consultation and consultation over particular important events that will affect the employment relationship – redundancy and transferring employees from different employers.

The Information and Consultation Regulations (2004) ensure that employers provide information to, and consult with, employees, but is only triggered when employees ask for an Information and Consultation Agreement. Employees and employers can agree what form the information and consultation is to take. The standard Information and Consultation provisions in S20 (1) enforce the communication of information concerning:

- The recent and probable development of the organization and the financial situation of the company.
- The situation, structure and probable development of employment within the undertaking and any anticipatory measures envisaged and whether there was a threat to employment.
- Any decisions which are likely to change the work organization or contractual relations, such as collective redundancies and transfer of undertakings.

Whilst the ICE regulations (2004) relate to more general information and consultation, the next two pieces of law cover particular circumstances.

The Transfer of Undertakings (Protection of Employment) Regulations (2006) requires employers to inform employees when a part of the business is outsourced or when a part of the business changes hands. For example, in-house cleaners can be transferred from the company to a provider who will provide services to clean the company. In this case the employment relationship has transferred to the provider of cleaning services. The regulations at S13 (2) ensure that affected employees, through their elected representatives, are informed of:

- The fact that the transfer is to take place, the date of the transfer and the reasons for it.
- The legal, economic and social implications for the affected employees.
- The measures that are (or are not) expected to take place in connection with the transfer, in relation to the affected employees.

The Trade Union and Labour Relations Consolidation Act (1992) provides for information and consultation to be undertaken when collective redundancies are being made. Collective redundancy consultation is dealt with in more detail in the companion book (**HR Fundamentals: Employment Law**).

These laws provide a structure for the areas of information and consultation that are viewed as vital to employees. Therefore, an organization has a legal requirement to meet its obligations to communicate on these matters. There is no legislative foundation for other aspects of communication and consultation, but the argument for good communication does not need a legal foundation; it is just good business.

Conflict

We can at times find that, despite our attempts to encourage communication, our time is taken up in reacting to conflict situations. In Chapter 1 we explained that the circumstances for conflict arising may occur when employees, either as different groups or as individuals, feel that their interests may be disadvantaged. Conflict also occurs when individuals hold differing views or ideas.

The role of conflict in innovation

It may be thought unusual to promote conflict as a method of innovation but without different opinions we cannot improve and develop ideas or products. The HR professional has a role here to encourage discussion of conflicting ideas, to help build an environment where the views of employees are valued and compliance is less important than creativity and innovation.

'*Creativity and innovative thinking* [are the] *means by which ideas are born and nurtured*' (Adair and Thomas, 2004: 1). But whilst creativity is the development of ideas, innovation is the application of those ideas into reality. Innovation is '*the intentional introduction and application within a role, group or organization of ideas, processes, products or procedures, new to the relevant unit of adoption, designed to significantly benefit the individual, the group, the organization or wider society*' (West and Farr, 1990: 9). In the Service and Manufacturing Sectors both creativity and innovation are needed to ensure that what is provided is unique so that competitiveness is sustained. For manufacturing industries, innovation is easier to view as the product is tangible and an example of innovation may be the provision of special features in the product. In the Service Sector, innovation covers both what is being offered and the way in which it is offered – an example of this is banking, where a change in technology ensures that customers can access their accounts online 24 hours a day. Whilst technology has made an important impact on business, innovation extends further than the development of new products or services. It may involve the use of technology or changes in the organization of work. And it extends beyond the boundaries of the business to innovative alliances made between businesses, methods of marketing and logistics.

Conflict impacts both on the process of creativity and the implementation of innovation and the role conflict plays in both will be covered. As most HR professionals and Line Managers know, conflict can be destructive when it concerns the relationships between colleagues or the process and resources available. However, cognitive conflict, the conflict between colleagues concerning the content of the task, is of particular interest. As mentioned in Chapter 1, conflicts over the task can lead to improvements in ways of working.

FIGURE 2.1   The Five Conflict Styles on Two Dimensions (after Thomas & Kilmann, 1974 in Badke-Schaub, Goldschmidt and Meijer, 2010)

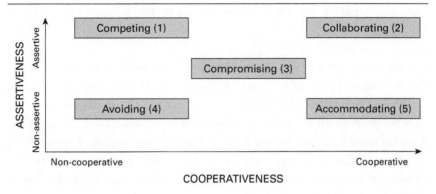

Employees have choices when there is a conflict, and there are five possible responses. Collaboration can be the most effective response (Weingart and Jehn, 2000). Conflicting ideas or viewpoints prompt employees to think flexibly and work together to explore options and attempt to identify new solutions that might meet the needs of all the team. Collaborative working, along with competition and compromise may be useful in the development of products. New ideas need to be expressed, and at times ideas shared together as a compromise; this can bring the best aspects of the two ideas together (Badke-Schaub, Goldschmidt and Meijer, 2010). Finally, a climate that accepts conflicting viewpoints is critical in the enhancement of creativity.

Conflict can also occur when innovative ideas are implemented, particularly when this involves improvements in the way organizations work. Whilst the process of creativity may not impact on the future of the team, implementing innovative ideas involves change. For example:

- consulting with members of another department;
- taking on additional tasks; or
- using different administrative processes.

This type of conflict, which is resistance to change, is a challenge to Line Managers and HR professionals alike. Some resistance to change will be a logical identification of problems with the new process. However, other reasons for such resistance may be fear of the impact of the change on existing ways of working, or fear of change itself. Some changes may be useful for the organization but result in an increased workload for employees. Other changes may require training for employees, and resistance to change is the result of anxiety over the employees' ability to manage.

It is plain that conflict should not be avoided and that the response to conflict is natural, but a disagreement is uncomfortable for many individuals. Line Managers will need to build a climate of trust where the team is open to other people's ideas so that creativity can be encouraged (Paulus, 2000). It is also suggested that, having built and maintained such an environment, the management of change may be easier as the environment exists for employees' views to be expressed and heard, and this may mean that issues do not fester and become formal grievances.

Cost of conflict – individual and collective

It is also apparent that conflict can have negative consequences, with a damaging effect on trust and respect between colleagues. For new teams it is recognized that there may be some conflict at first as norms and rules of working are determined (Tuckman, 1965). However, continued disagreements about resources and personal disagreements between team members can disrupt the team and is not conducive to effective team-work. Initially, Line Managers and latterly HR professionals may be asked to intervene in interpersonal conflict or conflict within a team. However, disagreement can also be between an individual and the organization and when this occurs there is a formal resolution mechanism – the grievance procedure.

The availability of a grievance procedure provides the employee with access to a mechanism to voice complaint and to resolve conflict. It also provides access to justice if the employee believes that the behaviour of the organization has been unfair. This is of value to the individual, but not all disagreements or complaints turn into a formal grievance. Employees may avoid taking action or they may accommodate whatever has changed without making a grievance. The issue may not be resolved but the individual has chosen not to escalate it. It may even be that the employee may choose to resign rather than to use the option available to seek redress – and that a formal grievance may only provide closure on the conflict rather than restore the employment relationship (Pruitt and Kim, 2004).

Research has shown that employees will act to restore freedoms that have been lost and whether they make a grievance is also related to whether or not they attribute the lost freedom to personal or environmental causes. If a freedom is lost and they attribute it to a decision of the organization, then the individual is more likely to make a grievance (Gordon and Bowlby, 1989). They may be more likely to make a grievance if their perception of the reliance the organization has on the employee is high – if they believe the organization needs them (Cappelli and Chauvin, 1991). This may indicate the motivation for employees to make a grievance. It shows that the decision to make a formal grievance is dependent on a number of factors. The issue and the chance of resolving it and retaining their position are all critical to the employee.

It is difficult to estimate the cost to individuals of expressing a conflict with the organization through a grievance. Employees may feel that their chances of promotion or pay rises may be reduced as they might be viewed as a trouble-maker, or that when a redundancy situation occurs they may be selected. It could be thought that by being identified as less than totally loyal they may affect their future prospects.

The cost of industrial action is easier to estimate. In the UK during August 2012, there were 10,000 working days lost from 15 stoppages and in the 12 months to August 2012, there were 1.25 million working days lost from 127 stoppages (Office for National Statistics, 2012). This gives a measure of the impact on the Gross National Product. However, the cost of strike action on individual businesses is profound. For example, the car manufacturer Hyundai ended a strike in South Korea which cost it £1.7 trillion in lost production (BBC, 2012).

For businesses the costs of industrial action are more than just the financial loss of potential production. The reputation of the company may have been damaged and any prospective new customers may have chosen more reliable suppliers. Within the organization, the violation of the psychological contract breeds an atmosphere of mutual mistrust, which may take some time to resolve. What was a close team now consists of employees who supported the industrial action and those that adamantly opposed it. These costs must have a financial but unmeasured impact, as the lack of engagement and continual low-grade disagreement and mistrust makes teams ineffective and inefficient.

The negative effects of conflict on individuals, teams, businesses and nationally are high. Line Managers and HR professionals play a key role to manage and reduce conflict so that teams can function.

The following case study looks in more detail at research carried out by the CIPD into developments in employee relations and collective dispute resolution. It is particularly encouraging to see improved relationships between Trade Unions and employers.

CASE STUDY Current Employee Relations and Trade Unions practices in the UK

A recent report from the CIPD (2012d) has indicated that employee relations have changed, with the imposition of industrial action becoming less common, despite the image given in the UK national press. Over the last 20 years the average number of days lost has been under 1 million, compared to 12.9 million in the 1970s and 7.2 million in the 1980s. When this is compared to the 131 million days lost in sickness absence in 2011 it puts the effect of industrial action into context.

Though stoppages have reduced this does not imply that the role of Trade Unions in collective conflict has also reduced. Trade Unions use other techniques, such as demonstrations, threatening to ballot to strike in order to encourage employers to negotiate, and causing damage to the employer brand.

HR now spends time trying to prevent conflict rather than to manage it. In the CIPD report, relationships were often positive and organizations strove to treat Unions as stakeholders:

> We have a good relationship with the Trade Unions. We have daily contact. I wouldn't resist use of the term 'partnership': we try to move forward in agreement, so far as that's possible. We give them lots of information; we involve them in everything we're doing; we aim to have 'no surprises'. It makes for a more effective change process and avoids a good deal of frustration. We refer to the Trade Unions more as key stakeholders than partners now, but, overall, it's the strength of the relationship that determines how well we do business together rather than the label we attach to it.
>
> (Dave Fitzgerald, BT)

However that was not always the theme, as Chris Haselden, Director of People and Leadership, Devon and Cornwall Police, and Chair, CIPD Police Forum explained:

> Now there is more resistance to change, less acceptance of new ways and more protective attitudes. Police officers have always shown goodwill by putting in extra hours, helping their local community in their own time, finishing off paperwork after their shift has ended and generally going the extra mile for the public. Now this discretionary effort has been undermined. While many officers are still doing these things, others are reacting to changes and quick to find fault. Their negativity is noticeable.

Chris Haselden explains how this is managed through good leadership and people management.

Conclusion

We at times are in a difficult situation, between the demands of the business, the wishes of managers and the needs of employees. We have a responsibility to ensure that we protect the business by ensuring it complies with legislation, but we also need to behave ethically. Good Employee Relations may not be easy when meeting all these demands. This chapter has shown that Employee Relations is important because it focuses both on the employer and the employee – getting the best for both parties whilst retaining a good relationship and reputation. It has also emphasized the value of Employee Relations in conflict management, whether it be managing disputes or promoting open communication to support an environment it which innovation will grow. We have looked at how Employee Involvement and Participation can influence an organization's performance, and this is now illustrated by the case study below.

In the following chapter we will take a strategic perspective, evaluating the impact of different variables on the choices we have when aligning Employee Relations strategy to the business.

CASE STUDY   Circle

Circle, a healthcare organization in the UK with an annual turnover of £80 million in 2009, comprising of practitioners, professionals and clinicians, manages hospitals and treatment centres. Disenchanted with the distance between consultant and patient, Circle was established to exceed patient expectations through excellence.

Circle has taken an approach to involvement, participation, voice and engagement that has six strands. These are as follows:

- The Ownership of Circle.

- Recruitment.

- Management and leadership.

- Decision-making.

- Voice.

- Reward.

Circle is a co-owned partnership with 49.9 per cent owned by clinicians and the rest by their employees – its partners. It gives clinicians the power to push the boundaries of experience and excellence on behalf of their patients (Circle, 2011). In fact, ownership of Circle has been extended to all employees, to reflect the fact that the patient experience of healthcare has broadened to include more than their relationship with the clinician. Ownership is something that has been approved of by the UK Government and is thought to encourage both a long-term view by employees together with greater commitment. This type of financial participation acts as an incentive to employees to participate fully in the business, with the rights and benefits of a shareholder.

Partners of Circle are involved in the recruitment process. Not only are they seeking employees that will go beyond what is stated in their job description but the selection process itself ensured that partners in the organization had decision-making power.

The leadership model proposed by Circle ensured that, instead of command and control being held at a bureaucratic centre, each business service was responsible for its own performance and success. This empowered employees to make direct improvements to patient care, by increased effort, innovation or continuous development. This model ensured that management was not 'faceless' and both improved employee voice and communication.

Day-to-day decision-making was moved away from management and to those who delivered the service. However, to enable effective decision-making employees needed correct and up-to-date information, and the appropriate skills and support. Information was openly distributed, including patient feedback, performance targets results and data on the financial performance of the business. The level of responsibility and autonomy for employees is more than within the more bureaucratic NHS and was initially unnerving, but the ability to make decisions also helped build engagement as employees supported the decisions that they had contributed towards. As a result of the culture of delegation and decision-making, employees and managers began to increase focus on employee communication; an employee magazine was started.

Individual employees were able to influence day-to-day decision-making on service delivery and to participate in wider discussions about the organization. At the individual level a strong relationship between employee and manager supported employee voice and employees felt listened to. At some sites collective voice was also brought about, such as an employee forum.

Circle employs directly or seconds employees from the NHS, and so the reward structure and content may differ, as seconded employees have their terms and conditions protected. Circle is working towards local pay determination, with budgets to reward and incentivize performance.

The example of participation and involvement that Circle gives shows not just the individual options that a company has for engaging with their employees but how an organization can incorporate these approaches. The culture and values of employee involvement is integral to Circle and its service delivery. Its approach has developed a collaborative partnership of professionals working to improve healthcare delivery.

This case study has been adapted from research carried out by IPA (Jameson, 2011).

Employee Relations and strategy

INTRODUCTION

Line Managers often have some understanding of business strategy. They are viewed as part of the operations, have an eye to developing their career to a more strategic role and may be in contact with those managers that influence business strategy. Conversely, many HR professionals have not been lucky enough to have exposure to business strategy. They often mix with other HR professionals, resulting in good practical knowledge of HR areas of responsibility but limited business knowledge. However, with the emphasis on strategic HRM and the role of HR as a business partner (Ulrich, 1997) we cannot jeopardise the profession by taking an inward-looking perspective.

HR professionals need to understand the strategy of a company and the strategy of their own HR department if they are to effectively make the right long-term strategic choices about how Employee Relations will be practised in that business. To help us understand this we will be looking at the strategic choices that we as HR professionals have to make and will be:

- determining the difference between corporate, business unit and operational strategy;
- discovering the effects of the Universalist and Contingency approaches to HR strategy;
- discussing the role of culture, values and lifecycles on strategy;
- evaluating the choices that are available to HR professionals in terms of representation, conflict resolution and EIP methods.

Reviewing business strategy

Strategy is the long-term direction of the organization. It is important for us to understand the planned direction that the organization is taking so that we can understand the decisions made by the organization. We can then calculate how this may impact on us as employees and our department. We will also see the impact that business strategy may have on HR, HR Strategy and the formulation of Employee Relations strategy.

Levels of business strategy

Organizations have to make choices about:

- the type of business that they are in;
- their range of products and services;
- how to sell these products or services competitively;
- who their customers may be.

Decisions are made on corporate and business level strategy. At the operational level decisions need to be made on how these strategies are delivered, and this is where HR strategy steps in.

Corporate level strategy

At the corporate level, the organization will need an overall strategy or direction. It will need to formulate its mission, from which the range of products will be clear. For example, NIKE has a portfolio of businesses covering sportswear, sports shoes, equipment and accessories. Their mission is '*to bring inspiration and innovation to every athlete in the world*' (NIKEINC, 2011a) and this limits their business to the sports sector (though they have some affiliated organizations that have widened the scope into the fashion industry). It is at corporate level that the geographic scope is also decided; whether an organization supplies its products or services locally, nationally, regionally or globally. NIKE, a MNC providing products worldwide, has its world headquarters in the United States, and regional headquarters in the Netherlands, China and Japan to enable it to sell its products worldwide (NIKEINC, 2011b).

The corporate level strategy determines the type of business the organization is in. This determines some aspects of Employee Relations strategy. For example if the organization is part of the UK aerospace industry, it is likely to use collective representation and recognize Unite and the GMB Unions. This is because, within the larger organizations in the British aerospace industry, these unions are recognized and employees moving between employers will bring an expectation of this practice with them.

The diversity of products and services and the company's geographic reach only provide part of the direction that is necessary, and there is a need to identify a long-term direction at a business unit level to sustain competitive advantage.

Business level strategy

A business unit is the smallest part of an organization that is responsible for producing a product or service. It has a market which is distinct from other business units in the organization and therefore has different customers, competitors and distribution channels than other business units. As a distinct entity the business unit will need to have its own view of its long-term direction, its strategy, to ensure that it takes hold of and maintains competitive advantage.

At business unit level a competitive strategy needs to be developed. To gain competitive advantage the unit may choose one of the following strategies, as described by Porter (1985):

- lead on price, providing cheap products whilst maintaining quality;
- lead on differentiation, selling its products or services with different features or benefits to the customer but with a higher price.

If the business has a low price strategy then this will impact on the choice of Employee Relations strategy. Tight control over resources needs to be taken, performance will be measured closely and there is little scope for generous employee pay or benefits. If the product price is to be low then to ensure profit, efficiencies need to be made. There are two options for organizations making this choice, depending on whether the organization values participation or control.

If participation is valued, employees may be asked to contribute, and this has been successful in many Japanese firms. For example the process of 'lean manufacturing', used by Toyota in their Production System, has an overarching principle to reduce waste in all processes (Basu and Miroshnik, 1999) with the only acceptable cost being one which adds value to the customer. Such approaches as lean manufacturing, Kaizen or Total Quality Management encourage problem solving through multi-functional teams; this will promote employee participation and involvement, and ultimately engagement. However, the Employee Relations strategy will also involve maintaining control when determining wages and other businesses with 'no frills' business strategies and a more autocratic management style may not choose to engender such employee engagement through participation.

Those businesses that follow a differentiation competitive strategy will need employees that focus on innovation and quality. An Employee Relations strategy that fosters innovation will have good communication, both upward and downward, promote employee voice and will have processes in place for employee involvement and participation. The organization would have developed a structure that enhanced co-ordination, collaboration and team-work. Organizations identified as innovative include Amazon.com, the online retail business, Danone, the French food company, and Baidu, the Chinese computer services firm, (Forbes, 2012).

Operational level strategy

This is the direction that the different operations develop in order to ensure that the business and corporate strategies are achieved. For HR it is the HR strategy and subsequent specialist strategies that needs to be aligned to the business and corporate strategy. Aligning HR strategies to the business makes sure that they all work towards the achievement of the business; they should also align rather than conflict with each other. For example, if the business needs to create innovative products, then the reward strategy should reward innovation and teamwork, and Employee Relations strategy should promote voice and participation.

The case study below makes us think hard about the theories that we have proposed. Amazon.com has been identified as an innovative company and as such should have progressive Employee Relations processes. However we can see from the case study that theoretical models provide a simplistic view and that organizations are complex.

CASE STUDY   Strategies for growth: Amazon

Amazon evolved from the dot-com investment crash to develop an innovative business strategy, using what was then a radical business model of online retailing to transform the staid book industry. It is a fast-moving competitive business, defending its position aggressively and moving into new markets quickly. One of the key strengths for Amazon has been its ability to move into 'white space' – those areas within the market where competitors are sparse but they can forecast relatively strong customer demand. Its customers have to be competent IT users to purchase online and so its move into a range of tablets has logic and there is an already substantial supply chain. Its mission is *'to be Earth's most customer-centric company for four primary customer sets: consumers, sellers, enterprises, and content creators'* (Amazon, 2011). It has moved from website retailer, to e-commerce partner (providing the ability for others to use the e-platform to access a wider customer base), to development platform from its establishment in 1995.

This rapid change should require communication and commitment, and a dynamic work environment which promotes involvement and participation. And at first view it could be thought that Amazon fits this – Forbes (2012) identifies Amazon as innovative. Yet its business strategy suggests that there are different requirements from different departments. Working as a picker and packer in a distribution centre, the customer-focused organization will need you to pick and pack as quickly as possible. This may be a very physically demanding role, one that is unlikely to be well-paid and should be relatively easy to fill. Rugeley, a coal-mine town in the UK which has not recovered from the closure of the pits, has an Amazon distribution warehouse. Here employees are paid barely the minimum wage, many are agency workers, work is intense and job security is poor (FT, 2013). A similar picture is given in Germany, where Amazon has been having difficulty with a union over pay and the use of temporary staff. As a Union official described it *'Everything is measured, everything is calculated, everything is geared toward efficiency. People want to be treated with respect.'* (The New York Times, 2013.)

So how does this fit with the view of Amazon as innovative, with an operation level strategy that rewards innovation and teamwork? Within many manufacturing organizations, warehouse picking and packing is a demanding and low-paid existence. Amazon does encourage other workers to be creative with their 'just do it' awards, and the fact that they do not use representation mechanisms, such as Employee Works Councils, unless there is a legal obligation for them to do so (Amazon, 2012) may not be enough evidence to support an unsettling feeling that, instead of innovative, it holds a low-cost business strategy.

Many of their specialist employees are in demand and work in a challenging, dynamic and creative environment – it would be reasonable to provide an open and engaging work environment that retains these valuable staff. Amazon have focussed on customers' needs and then met them, owning projects, taking risks – making a difference. There is little information on the relationship between more specialist employees and Amazon, and this may be an area that could be beneficial for Amazon to promote in the light of its more recent bad press in 2013. It is unclear that Amazon's Employee Relations for its specialist employees does use the necessary approaches for the future of the company. It is suggested that an alternative is that the founder, CEO Jeff Bezos, has a strong presence and that he is driving the decisions within Amazon. If this is the case and the culture is authoritative, then there is little fostering of innovation from these staff. They will therefore put Amazon on their CV as a well-known and profitable business and move onto other work. Without a participative and innovative team environment reliance on the CEO will continue, with higher staff turnover and no succession planning. If this is the case the future of Amazon depends solely on Jeff Bezos.

Reviewing HR strategy

Before we go on to discuss HR Strategy it is important to explain the different approaches that can be taken. There are two different HR Strategy philosophies and these are the Universalist and Contingency approaches.

The Universalist approach suggests that there are key HR practices that are more effective than others. Pfeffer (1994) sets out 16 key practices, or bundles of practices, that should be incorporated. A large number of these relate to the Employee Relations strategy and include:

- job security;
- high wages;
- incentive pay;
- employee ownership;
- information sharing;
- participation and empowerment;
- teamwork and cross-utilization;
- symbolic egalitarianism;
- wage compression.

By making sure that employees feel that there is equality and a reduction in formality and by ensuring that team work is encouraged by compressing wages (so reducing individual competition), Pfeffer (1994) argues that these practices will improve competitive advantage. But the Universalist approach to strategy imposes set practices and there is little interaction with employees. Though it is a valuable list for us as HR professionals, it does not take account of the other factors that influence HR strategy.

The Contingency approach has a closer link to business strategy, with the ability to adjust HR practices in line with a range of different circumstances rather than prescribing practices whatever the situation.

If we were to take the Universalist approach there would be little to discuss in terms of the impact of corporate values, culture or company life-cycles, as the practices that are suggested as the best to use do not alter. There also would be little alignment of HR policy and no choice of practice. Alternatively, with the Contingency approach different circumstances, such as business strategy, lifecycle or type of business, will affect the type of practice chosen. We will now go on to discuss the circumstances that may affect the choice of HR strategy.

Impact of company lifecycle on HR strategy

HR Strategy may need to differ depending on the stage of 'life' an organization has reached (Kochan and Barocci, 1985). These stages are shown below:

FIGURE 3.1   Lifecycle of an organization

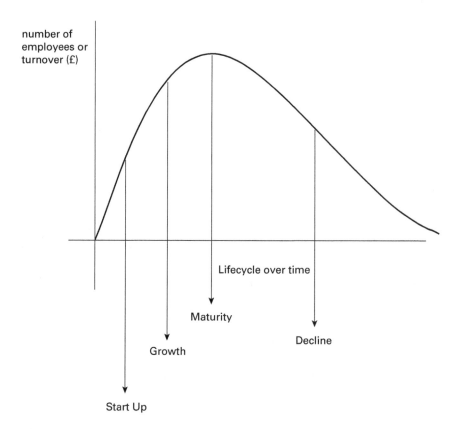

Start-up stage

At the start-up stage HR practices may be limited. For the organization survival is important. Time and effort is expended to recruit the talent and the financial reward for such talented employees may be high. The organization needs to be as flexible as possible and often the business strategy is emergent, rather than planned, as opportunities for business development arise and are taken. In this working environment innovation skills are valued and employees are encouraged to participate and be involved. Often the team is very small and the structure and employment relationship informal and individualistic in nature; formal policies are rare. However it is at this time that the core values and mission of the organization is established and the founder of the organization may have an important role in creating the environment and expectations for Employee Relations.

This description of a prospector start-up organization may not be appropriate for all SMEs. It also suggests that in this high-risk participative environment Employee Relations is similar in all small businesses but in reality the range of Employee Relations strategies is broad. Some small newly formed organizations are autocratic, others very participative. Despite this disparity in Employee Relations strategic approaches, most small organizations lack resources and, therefore, will have an unexpressed Employee Relations strategy which is informal and individualistic.

Growth stage

In the UK there are many SMEs; some of these will always remain small but a proportion will be successful and grow. As the organization develops the distance between the individual employee and management will grow. In the beginning, the small team will have good communication as a result of the small networks required to pass on information. In the growth phase communication is more difficult and employees can feel isolated from adequate information: practices need formalizing, including communication. As a start-up there was little need (or time) for formal team meetings; now there are department meetings and even written minutes.

It is as the organization grows that the need for HR becomes apparent – often an existing employee widens their role to take on HR responsibilities and eventually they become externally trained and set up a new HR department. Alternatively trained HR professionals are recruited to take on this role. Either situation can be difficult; for the existing member of the team credibility is a challenge as they need to be viewed as an HR professional in their new role. For a newly recruited HR professional to establish a new department can be difficult as existing employees do not necessarily understand the need. Both types of new HR professionals in a growth organization can find they take an administrative expert role (Ulrich, 1997) and struggle over time to gain consent for HR to contribute to its full potential. Initially their role is to make HR practices and policies precise, transparent and written, and to protect the company from Employment Tribunal claims. The Employee Relations strategy can be one of the last parts of HR to become formalized, particularly if the employment relationship remains individualistic in nature. However gradually Employee Relations strategy becomes more formal and there is a need to maintain stability, reduce conflict and motivate employees.

The Employment Relations strategy chosen will differ with other factors influencing the company. In some sectors, such as manufacturing, it may be now that employees seek collective representation. It is usually not an actual strategic decision made by management. It could be because of employees' experience of collective representation whilst they have been working in other companies or it may be common within the industry. As the organization grows it is harder for the Managers to maintain a good employment relationship with all employees and employees could feel that the organization does not value them and that they need to be represented by a Union.

Maturity stage

At the maturity stage control is very important. The need to control costs results in restrictions in pay, and this may result in some employees leaving. This is actually of benefit as some employee turnover is required to reduce the need for redundancies. The Employee Relations strategy, whilst attempting as always to reduce conflict, also needs to increase productivity. This is in its own way a method of cost reduction and there is increased pressure on the pay–effort bargain. It is a balance as increased control and cost reduction may cause increased conflict.

Decline stage

At the decline stage, redundancies and increased turnover of employees is expected as the demand for the product or services of the organization reduces. At this stage Employee Relations concentrates on reducing conflict but redundancies inevitably are resisted by Trade Unions and there may be some collective disputes as the state of the business becomes apparent to employees. Comet, the UK electrical appliances retailer, struggled to survive in November 2012, with redundancies the first line of defence (*The Guardian*, 2012). Many firms are thought to be surviving just because the interest payments on business loans are so low (*The Financial Times*, 2013) and in the UK it is expected that there will be increased failures with increasing interest charges.

Impact of corporate values and culture on HR strategy

Organizational culture is the shared assumptions that have been learnt by the group to solve problems and are taught to new employees as the correct ways to perceive, think and feel in relation to the problems (Schein, 1985). It can be seen as the values, beliefs, behaviours and assumptions that employees within an organization possess.

If the behaviours, thoughts, feelings, values and beliefs that employees will exhibit are those that reinforce and support the business strategy, then the organization's culture supports that strategy. However, when the strategy needs to change, then cultural aspects need to adapt to ensure that the strategy is supported. HR strategy may contribute to culture change through the use of reward strategies to incentivize new desirable behaviour. It may be that Employee Relations strategy changes to build in particular approaches that are desired as part of the new HR strategy. Finally it is important to ensure that the values that are demonstrated in the HR strategy are those that the organization would endorse.

Aligning employee relations strategy

It is most practicable in today's modern working environment to take a contingency approach and to ensure that HR strategy is aligned with the corporate and business strategies of the company. This enables all the policies and practices to focus on the key deliverables. Employee Relations strategy originates from both the business strategy and HR strategies, and should relate closely to other policies and practices. For example a business strategy that prizes innovation will require a Reward strategy that incentivizes creativity and an Employee Relations strategy that provides open communication and opportunities for true participation and involvement.

Three different Employee Relations practices are now discussed as strategic choices.

Choices – representation and recognition

In the past, employers have perceived the choice to be between individual or collective representation. However, the employment relationship cannot be effectively established and sustained through an intermediary – even where collective representation is available the company will relate to the individual at particular times. And there is no legal requirement for an employer to choose collective representation and to recognize a Union. In the UK there has been a history of voluntarism; the freedom for employer and employee to decide on how they are to carry out their relationship rather than have Parliament enforce it through legislation.

Collective representation can enable a consistent and endorsed message to be passed to employees, which may benefit the organization: employees can make their views known without being identified.

However, Trade Unions are not the sole method of collective representation. Employee forums, consultative committees and European Work Councils are all available for organizations to use with or without resorting to the use of Union representation. Under the European Works Councils Directive (No 2009/38) elected employees in MNCs have the right to be informed and consulted about transnational issues, such as mergers and cross-border restructuring.

As always, the selection made will depend on the circumstances, and in particular the contents of the corporate and business strategies – national factors, including national history and culture, social trends and employment legislation also affect that choice. In the United States, collective representation is very much on the decline, at 11 per cent in the private sector as at 1995 (James, 1995), and despite a commission to review the employment relationship the role of Union collective representation was the only one expressed (USDLC, 1994). Therefore, in the United States there is predominately individual employee representation. This is also particularly apt in a country where individuals and their rights prevail. In New Zealand and Australia there is a greater acceptance of Unions; legislative changes in New Zealand have led to a greater number of Unions (though it is arguable whether they are truly Unions) (Barry and May, 2004). In Germany there is a dual system of Union representation and Works Councils (Weiss, 2004).

Choices – management of conflict and dispute resolution

When making a strategic choice on managing conflict an employer is communicating its values to its employees. These choices show the value placed on the employment relationship and justice for the employee. For example, if an employer's grievance procedure is fair, carried out by appropriately trained managers and with the opportunity to appeal, then this communicates to employees that they will be listened to. This does not mean that at each grievance the employer will always agree with the employee, but that the employer takes the process seriously. An employer can made strategic choices on how to manage both individual and collective grievances, how to attempt to reduce conflict and how to manage conflict when it extends beyond the bounds of the organization.

An organization has some little leeway over the grievance procedure as it is governed by law. In fact it would possibly be illegal if an employer changed the way it resolved individual conflict from using a grievance approach, where grievances are heard and investigated, to a mediation approach where both sides attempt to work through the problem without access to a grievance procedure. Where an organization has influence is over the nuances of the process, over how the grievance is carried out and with whom rather than the process itself. If the grievance was not resolved internally and the employee makes an Employment Tribunal claim for constructive dismissal, then the employer has more choices. Some employers make a strategic choice to settle all Employment Tribunal claims to prevent high legal costs, lengthy and time-consuming legal processes and any possible bad publicity. However this does communicate to employees (when this becomes known), that the employer may be at fault and also to unscrupulous employees that they have the ability to resign, claim constructive dismissal and make money out of the Employment Tribunal claim. Others chose to make any decision on settlement on a case by case basis, settling on legal advice, if the risk of losing is too high or when they are seen to be at fault. For settlement agreements see *HR Fundamentals: Employment Law* (Aylott, 2014).

When it comes to collective grievances, the procedure by which grievances are brought by the Union on behalf of its members will have been agreed by the organization as part of a collective agreement with the Union. This is an important grievance management process as for the employer it encourages the Union to discuss grievances rather than decide to take industrial action. If the grievance was not resolved internally both parties will have written into the collective agreement the steps that are to be taken. Often both parties will have to use a third party to resolve the conflict: in the UK this is ACAS. Employers usually choose for ACAS to provide collective conciliation but it also provides an arbitration service.

Finally employers do have some choice over any action they may take to reduce the possibility of conflict. Employers are most concerned over Employment Tribunal claims and may take steps to prevent claims by using compromise agreements. Employers make a strategic choice for when and with whom compromise agreements are used – some organizations will use them with redundancies, to prevent claims and reduce any unfavourable publicity over the redundancies by ensuring that the redundant employee keeps silent about the redundancy and any payment. Other organizations will only use compromise agreements for higher management. The choice of using compromise or settlement agreements prepared by lawyers gives employers peace of mind, but at a financial cost. Due to the nature of a settlement agreement employees are unlikely to know much about the practice in their workplace, but they may see employees leaving without any understanding of why. This makes for an uneasy and insecure workplace.

Choices – involvement and participation (EIP methods)

We have seen in Chapter 2 that communication can influence the performance of employees and the organization but that the link between participation and employee or organizational performance is less clear. Therefore it benefits an employer to choose to communicate to employees.

An employer has to make an initial decision about the existence of EIP methods, and then to take a further decision as to the extent to which these will be offered. This decision may be influenced by employment history, legislation and social attitudes. However when it comes to participation measures, the supply and demand of labour influences the choice of participation. If there is a shortage of employees then employers need to attract labour, and to do this they work towards being Employers of Choice. Having methods by which employees have a voice and can participate, can improve engagement and so attract and retain employees in a difficult labour market. However if there is little demand for labour there is less need for organizations to spend both time and money on attracting and retaining employees, and so employers may chose to limit the use of participation and involvement. During times of low labour demand, when either there is an economic crisis affecting the labour market as a whole, or the organization is in the decline stage of the lifecycle, it is more important for businesses to spend their resources on survival and communicating to employees about redundancy and job insecurity.

Conclusion

Whilst corporate strategy may be explicit, and communicated down to employees, business strategy is not always clearly communicated. In fact not all business strategy is deliberate and as a result of clear decision-making. In fast-paced and start-up organizations, business strategies may emerge as opportunities arise and circumstances change. In public sector organizations, business strategy is traditionally deliberate and therefore it is easier to align Employee Relations strategy to this. In the private sector, even when the business strategy is clearly communicated, we often do not plan ahead and fail to co-ordinate the HR strategy to provide a coherent approach across all the specialisms including Employee Relations. In this case unfortunately a reactive and fire-fighting approach is taken to Employee Relations with little consistency or rationale.

The first few chapters have provided a broad basis on which to found our knowledge of Employee Relations. We now move towards the practice of Employee Relations, with the next chapter explaining how Employee Relations works.

CASE STUDY   Nationality and Employee Relations strategy

The scope for Employee Relations is set by the geographic boundaries of the organization and this case study reviews the impact of nationality on Employee Relations strategy. We compare two countries, the United States and Germany, and their approach to Employee Relations.

Germany, with its incorporation of the European Social Model, has a dual model of representation, with representation by Unions and also the use of Work Councils established by law. In common with many other European countries it does not recognize individual employee representation and collective bargaining is the predominant method of changing terms and conditions through the Works Councils. Works Councils also have codetermination, whereby a proportion of employee representatives have seats on the supervisory board and have influence over key employment issues, such as recruitment and promotion. This centralized approach makes change within organizations slow but systematic and thorough. For both employer and employee alike it gives security and stability. But when it comes to making strategic choices the German government has actually provided legislation that enforces the social model.

In the United States the decline in Union membership, at 11.8 per cent in 2011, (Bureau of Labor Statistics, 2012) and reduction in Union power has altered Employee Relations. While there is limited collective bargaining in the United States, the employment relationship is more concerned with individual issues surrounding the employment contract. According to Wever (1995) in organizations where Unions represent employees, the Unions have control over how the job is structured and completed, more detailed influence than Work Councils, and this is why US employers vigorously resist Unionization. Employment protection is relaxed and this means that employers have the ability to hire and fire, managing the need for flexibility with greater ease than in Germany. The US approach provides the opportunity for employers to make choices on employment relations, with the ability to manage this unilaterally rather than by using negotiation (Wever, 1995).

It may seem that national institutions, the history of employment relations in each country, the legislative framework of employee relations and the views of each respective society dictate the choices made by US or German companies. This might be true of domestic firms but MNCs have greater scope. Whilst subsidiaries in other countries will be subject to local law, there may be scope to make some choices. For example, BMW and Mercedes Benz, both German companies, have chosen to be non-unionized at the US sites (Wever, 1995). For US firms working in Mexico, despite the employers' resistance to unionization the fact that Mexico is a more unionized labour market will influence the choices that US companies make (Greer and Stephens, 1996).

Employee Relations in many organizations is reactive and lacks a planned approach where it fits the business and HR strategy. This does not get the best from Employee Relations. The questionnaire below provides an opportunity for you to reflect on your own organization, your understanding of its strategy and how Employee Relations fits into this.

DIAGNOSTIC QUESTIONNAIRE   Strategy

	Yes	No
1 Has a corporate strategy been communicated widely?	☐	☐
2 Do you understand the corporate strategy?	☐	☐
3 Has the business strategy been communicated widely?	☐	☐
4 Do you understand the business strategy?	☐	☐
5 Is there an HR strategy?	☐	☐
6 Does it fit with the business strategy?	☐	☐
7 Does it fit with other operational strategies?	☐	☐
8 Do the different strategies match together?	☐	☐
9 Do the values of the HRM strategy match those of the business?	☐	☐
10 Does the ER strategy fit other HRM strategies?	☐	☐

Between 10 and 7 positive answers
Your organization has the ability to plan ahead and has a well-ordered approach to strategy development. This may be because of the experience of leadership in your organization, or the type of business that you operate in. You also have a logical and strategic HRM department which has prepared an HR strategy and has a proactive and strategic view of the role HR plays.

Between 6 and 4 positive answers
Your organization provides a clear corporate and business strategy but this is not always translated into HR strategy. Alternatively, you have an operationally focused organization and HR department. However to enable the strategy to be realized these need to be developed further.

Between 4 and 2 positive answers
Your organization has a degree of strategy but may not communicate it effectively. Alternatively, your HRM department has forward-thinking ideas but is not always viewed strategically. The HRM department has difficulty being included in planning strategy and so the parts of strategy are distinct and not integrated effectively. Over time HR professionals need to be viewed as more proactive and able to effectively contribute to the business.

IN PRACTICE

Employee Relations in practice

04

INTRODUCTION

HR is vital in the communication of the values of your organization – through the policies and procedures it communicates to employees and management, through the actions it shows are acceptable (and those that are not and will be subject to discipline), and through how it treats people while attempting to do business and to make a profit. In this chapter we will be looking at the methods that HR professionals use to manage some of the key areas of Employee Relations. We will:

- identify how an employer chooses effective EIP methods for their own situation;
- suggest ways to improve downward communication;
- review the need for and the actual mechanism of discipline and grievance procedures;
- discuss how collective bargaining and negotiation work:
  - Identify the procedure for Union recognition
  - Explain the process of industrial action
  - Describe what you should expect when dealing with possible industrial action.

Involvement and participation

There are a full range of EIP types that could be used. An employer could:

- communicate with employees using team briefs or in-house journals;

- consult with employees at appraisals and by using suggestion schemes; or

- enable employees to participate in decision-making at team level using quality circles or at company level using Employee Works Councils (EWC), Joint Consultative Committees (JCC) or Union representation.

We have seen in Chapter 3 some of the choices made by employers in line with business strategy. A further practical range of factors need to be taken into account when deciding on what types of involvement and participation should be undertaken, and these are shown below.

FIGURE 4.1   Factors influencing the choice of EIP approach

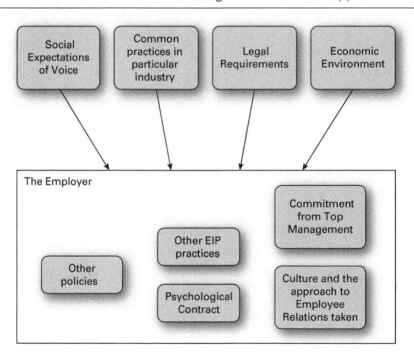

The employer's choice of EIP approaches depends on the expectations of society for voice – we mentioned in Chapter 1 how employees have become more assertive, with higher expectations of having a voice and being listened to. Employees with experience in certain industries are used to particular practices in terms of voice. In the UK the public sector is strongly unionized and collective voice is common. In the automotive sector with a few large global companies, Employee Works Councils (EWCs) are also common (Pedersini, 2003). GKN, the British car and aerospace components manufacturer, operates worldwide and uses an EWC (GKN, 2012). The choice of approach also relies on the economic environment (and therefore the need for EIP) and the legal requirements.

Within the organization a primary influence will be the organization's culture and values, and influenced by this the expectations of the employees through the psychological contract. When new Line Managers attempt to bring new approaches to involvement and participation they often bring their own past experience of what has worked well, without taking account of the culture of the organization and the expectations of employees.

Downward communication

At times the HR department is involved in communication to individuals, for example by letter to inform an employee of a pay rise or to a candidate informing them of success in a job application or face to face to Line Managers seeking advice. However, they also are responsible for communication to the whole company, be it by ensuring written details of job vacancies are posted on the intranet or by supporting Managers to communicate details of redundancies or a take-over.

Whether individual or corporate communication there are some key principles that should be carried out:

- identify the audience;
- recognize the needs of the audience;
- identify the message and media to be used;
- ensure a consistency of message if different media are used;
- ensure that the message that is communicated is consistent with organizational values;
- identify the response or actions sought from the audience;

- identify whether this is a one-off communication or a series of communications to different audiences;
- assess the effectiveness of the communication.

Let us examine this in a little more detail using two examples – a discipline letter and a communication about a collective redundancy.

A letter inviting an employee to a discipline meeting needs to be jargon-free. A relatively new employee, with little understanding of the business – one with English as a second language or a young person new to the world of work – will have different needs to a senior manager. A discipline letter has legal standing and it is important that assumptions are not made about the understanding. If there is any danger of the letter not being clearly understood we should arrange for their line manager or Trade Union representative to go through it with them. The employee receiving the letter will need to have:

- information on the reason for the disciplinary meeting and any accusation (so that the employee is able to effectively put together a defence and can answer the case with any available evidence);
- details of their right to be accompanied;
- information on the date of the meeting.

It is wise to use a traditional medium (eg post) with a message that this is a serious accusation, and an explanation of the possible consequences. If the employee needs to reply to state that they will attend or to rearrange, then it is important to identify the timeframe for this. This letter will be referred to during the meeting and a further letter will be prepared afterwards, with details of the results of the meeting and any sanction decided on (if appropriate). The reason for the disciplinary action and any accusation needs to be consistent in both letters.

The information about collective redundancy may comprise a wider audience, including:

- individuals at risk of redundancy;
- those who are part of the team;
- customers and suppliers and potential customers and suppliers, (particularly if the local press is involved); and
- the local community.

For HR the communication will concentrate on employees, both those immediately involved in the redundancy and those that could remain with the employer afterwards, but details of the communication may get to the press – and others within the company may be involved in managing press enquiries.

We recognize the challenge of such a difficult communication, and in some respects we cannot meet the need of all employees to know that they are not the ones that have been selected. But all employees need to know that they will be treated fairly and legally, whether selected for redundancy or not, and that they are valued by the employer, and where possible the employer will try to retain them or support them to move to another job. It might be that the message is 'we will do our best by you within the boundaries of what the business needs' and this needs to be communicated through team meetings, individual consultations and by letter.

As the 'at risk of redundancy' letter has different information to pass on, all with legal consequences, it may be difficult to retain the consistency of the overall message of the communication – that 'we are doing the best that we can within the boundaries of business need'. The aim of the letter is to ensure that individually employees know their rights, and this will also have been covered during the team brief, and at individual consultation meetings. The response required from employees is that they seek as much information and support as they need going forward in this process. Some employers may provide additional support, though this may depend on the number of employees being made redundant and the values of the organization.

To assess the effectiveness of the communication is difficult, but it may be measured in the number of enquiries seeking further information as the communication strategy was not clear or the number of grievances and Employment Tribunal claims. In this case the communication is consistent with a high emotion response and so it is difficult to measure the effectiveness of the communication in light of this. It may be that measuring 'collateral damage', retention over the next year may be a more accurate measure.

Conflict – individual dispute resolution

We now go on to assess the need for individual dispute resolution methods and how to manage these disputes. Individual dispute resolution could in reality just refer to grievance procedures but it seems reasonable to take this opportunity to deal with disputes with employees by the employer (covered by discipline and ultimately dismissal) as well as disputes by grievance (covered by grievance and ultimately resignation and a claim of constructive dismissal).

Grievance procedures

The need for grievance procedures

In Chapter 1, we discussed the imbalance of power in the employment relationship and the need of the employee to have the opportunity to voice complaints and to believe that they will be treated fairly. One method of employee voice is the grievance – grievances are 'concerns, problems and complaints that employees raise with their employers' (ACAS, 2009c: 3). So the grievance procedure can be viewed as a formal tool for employee voice, where, for example, employees may voice problems with other employees or their manager.

In the UK there is no legal statute that enforces grievance procedures. However ACAS has produced a Code of Practice which employers are expected to follow. Failure to follow the Code of Practice is taken account of by an Employment Tribunal if there is a claim against the company, but failure to follow the Code is not illegal in itself. If a Tribunal claim fails, an employer may find that their compensation payment to the claimant is up to 25 per cent higher due to not following the Code of Practice.

This does not mean we can advise employers that they have no legal requirement to have a grievance procedure as case law has determined that employers have the implied duty to provide a procedure to resolve disputes. In *W A Gould (Pearmak) Ltd v McConnell and anor* [1995] IRLR 516, the claimant had no clear process to make a formal grievance and there was no prospect of their complaint being resolved. Despite this, the Employment Tribunal agreed that they were right to resign and claim constructive dismissal.

The grievance process

FIGURE 4.2 The grievance procedure adapted from ACAS (2011)

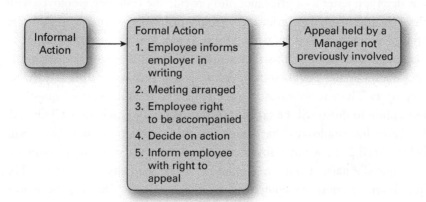

As the chart above suggests, employees should first attempt to resolve any grievance informally with their Line Manager, who will need to use their judgement as to whether this should be recorded. Employees often come to their Line Manager with requests, problems and complaints, many of which are inconsequential and quickly resolved. Others are more complex, serious or, despite the Line Manager's intervention, cannot be resolved; in these cases the Line Manager should make a record of the conversation and suggest to the employee that they make a formal grievance. As always any record of conversations should be dated and counter-signed by the employee.

However, complications arise for informal resolution of grievances with the Line Manager when the complaint involves this actual Line Manager. In these circumstances the grievance procedure should provide an alternative Manager for the employee, but in small organizations this may be difficult.

The Code of Practice sets out the steps of the procedure as follows:

- let the employer know the nature of the grievance;
- hold a meeting with the employee to discuss the grievance;
- allow the employee to be accompanied at the meeting;
- decide on appropriate action;
- allow the employee to take the grievance further if not resolved.

Making the grievance formal

To make a formal grievance the employee will put the complaint in writing so that the employer is aware of the main issues. We may need to interpret a resignation letter as a grievance and provide the resigning employee with the right to pursue their grievance. From April 2014 we may also find that employees may contact us with informal questions to support a claim of discrimination. Prior to this they would have sent a statutory discrimination questionnaire but these have been abolished to reduce the burden on employers. There is no statutory requirement to respond to these questions but failure to do so will be taken into account at an Employment Tribunal. However for employees that have a claim that refers to acts that occur before April 2014 we may find that we still receive a statutory discrimination questionnaire from an employee (s138, Equality Act 2010). The questionnaire must be completed by the employer. This questionnaire, or the informal questions, may be the first an employer knows of a complaint of discrimination by an employee and should be seen as a grievance letter.

When the employer receives details of the grievance in writing, the employer will invite the employee by letter to a meeting, where the employee will give further details of the grievance. The letter will inform the employee that they have the right to be accompanied by a companion (s10, Employment Relations Act 1999). The letter should be sent without delay and the subsequent meeting should be arranged as soon as is possible, usually within five working days. This ensures that the employee feels that the employer is taking the issue seriously.

The meeting

The Manager hearing the grievance will prepare by reading the letter, identifying if a similar grievance has been made by other employees and ensuring that the need for an interpreter or any reasonable adjustments are made if the employee is disabled, so that they can express their complaint without difficulty.

The first meeting enables the employee to explain the grievance and what they would like done to resolve the issue. The meeting will be held in a private office where the employee can speak freely without fear of interruption or being overheard. During the meeting the issues need to be examined, and it may be that by open discussion the issue may be resolved. For more complex issues the meeting may need to be adjourned to allow an investigation to be carried out. The companion can play a role in explaining issues on behalf of the employee. They may make the employee's case or summarize it or confer with the employee but cannot answer questions on behalf of the employee or prevent the employer from explaining the company's position.

The issue of a companion at grievance meetings has been problematic. Firstly the companion can be a fellow colleague or a Trade Union representative (s10 (3), Employment Relations Act, 1999). (Employees do not have the right to legal representation at grievance meetings.) Secondly employees have a right to a companion for grievances that involve a duty that the employer has for the employee, eg duty of care. However if the grievance does not have a duty covered by either case law or statute, then there is no legal requirement for a companion (ACAS, 2011). In practice this may be a difficult issue for the HR professional to determine and it is a wise choice to allow a companion to attend any grievance. In fact this allows for grievances that develop in the meeting to cover more than was initially laid out in the grievance letter. Finally companions have the right to protection against detriment or dismissal. This means that a person acting as a companion as part of a grievance cannot be disadvantaged or dismissed because of their involvement in the grievance. This protection means that fellow employees can provide support for others to voice a complaint without fearing any negative consequences.

Once all relevant details have been taken the employer will close the meeting and decide on an appropriate action. This may be to investigate further, in which case the employer will put this in writing to the employee. It may be that a decision on the grievance is made, and the employer will also put this in writing to the employee, with details of the appeals process so that the employee can access this if they wish to take the issue further.

The appeal

The appeal should be held as soon as possible with another more senior Manager. The invitation to the appeal should be in writing, with a reminder that they still have the right to be accompanied. The purpose of the appeal is:

- to determine whether the grievance process has been followed fairly;

- to assess whether any new evidence has become available and make appropriate decisions in light of any new evidence;
- to determine whether the decision is inherently unfair.

It may be that again further investigation is required before a final decision is given, in writing. The decision at the end of the appeal is final.

Constructive dismissal

At this stage we must briefly explain constructive dismissal, as many claims can be resolved at an early stage if the company deals effectively with a grievance.

In *Western Excavating (ECC) Ltd v Sharp* [1978] IRLR 27 the Court of Appeal described constructive dismissal as 'a significant breach going to the root of the contract of employment'. The claim of constructive dismissal can be made if there is a fundamental breach of the employment contract by the employer. For example, if an employer does not protect the employee from the retaliation of a Manager after a grievance has been brought, does not pay wages or makes an employee work in a dangerous environment without adequate protection. These may breach the implied trust and confidence an employee should be able to have in the employer. The employee will need to resign without delay to show that the breach has not been accepted and then make a claim for unfair constructive dismissal at an Employment Tribunal.

In *Hunter v Timber Components (Ltd)* [2009] UKEAT 0025/09 a joiner complained about the owner's son, who was a bully and had been appointed a Director. There had been a disagreement between the joiner and the owner's son about the owner's son shouting at another member of the team. The joiner went sick before resigning and claiming unfair constructive dismissal. In this case the claim was made despite the fact that the joiner was not subject to the bullying. The link between the joiner's illness and the bullying behaviour could not be substantiated so the claim failed.

Whilst the employee is protected in circumstances of fundamental breaches there are also situations when an employee experiences a series of acts in which the last one is the last straw. According to the Court of Appeal in *London Borough of Waltham Forest vs Omilaju* [2004] EWCA Civ 1493, the last straw may be a reasonable and justifiable act (in this case not paying the claimant for a day when he attended an Employment Tribunal for a claim he had against them). However, in most cases the last straw is a more extreme action by the employer which is not reasonable.

The case study below provides an example of a case that went to Employment Tribunal and Employment Appeal Tribunal and illustrates constructive dismissal.

CASE STUDY Employment Law on grievance

In the case below the organization applies its grievance policy consistently, but in doing so omits to manage a complaint concerning bias. Many HR Professionals will believe that by being consistent an employer is being fair – however, each case should be managed on its merit.

Watson v The University of Strathclyde (2011) IRLR 458, the claimant was a publishing officer, who had worked for the employer since 1985. Her immediate Manager was recruited in 2004. The claimant found her Manager's behaviour aggressive, unprofessional, intimidating and threatening and in 2006 made a grievance. This grievance was not upheld and she appealed. On the appeal panel was the Secretary of the University who had been responsible for supporting the claimant's Manager after an airgun incident for which the Manager had been convicted. The claimant requested that the Secretary should not be part of the panel. The University considered the request but refused to change the panel. The appeal failed.

The claimant resigned and claimed constructive dismissal. This was heard by the Glasgow Employment Tribunal and she failed in her claim, as it concluded that the Secretary would normally have participated in the appeal panel. However the Employment Appeal Tribunal (EAT) reviewed the case and suggested that the Employment Tribunal had erred in its decision. It decided that the University had failed in its duty of implied trust and confidence by including a member of the panel that the claimant viewed as biased towards her Line Manager.

The EAT had based its decision on a previous case, *Porter v Magill* (2002 2 AC 357), in which it was determined that any panel needs to be free from actual and apparent bias. The University was large enough to reconvene a panel for the appeal without difficulty. It was thought that any reasonable employer would consider the perception of justice in the appeal process and the perception of bias held by the claimant was enough for her to claim a fundamental breach to the duty of trust and confidence, and to successfully claim constructive dismissal.

Discipline procedures

The need for discipline procedures

The parties in an employment relationship have mutual obligations, and if the employee breaks their part of the obligation then the employer can use the discipline procedure. This can be uncomfortable for some Line Managers, who dislike having to confront their staff and others may feel that the discipline procedure is an excessively bureaucratic and blunt tool to use. Finally some Managers may be concerned about the legal implications of using the discipline procedure, particularly if it leads to dismissal. For whatever reason Line Managers may choose to ignore the problem. To disregard these problems undermines the authority and leadership of the individual Manager and the effectiveness of the business.

The consistent use of the discipline procedure enables the business to communicate to the employee what is acceptable and unacceptable behaviour or performance. This can provide the opportunity for employees to change and it can be argued that without this the procedure is unjust. Finally, if you follow the discipline procedure it protects the company as it shows that the company's decisions are measured and reasonable and that the process has been fair.

The Employment Rights Act (1996) s96 provides for employees to be dismissed for a range of reasons, which include conduct or capability. Though at the first incident or indication of a problem the employer is usually not thinking in terms of dismissal, it is important to identify whether the issue is one of conduct or capability as they are treated differently from the outset. There is a logical reason for the difference – if it is misconduct the employee has a responsibility to change their behaviour; if it is capability due to poor performance the employee may need support and training to improve, and if it is capability due to sickness a different approach is needed altogether.

Usually the discipline procedure deals with misconduct and capability due to poor performance. Issues of conduct include for example the use of abusive language, the use of drugs, disobedience or dishonesty. However, other policies such as that covering the use of alcohol and drugs or the internet policy will also need to be referred to. Absence is a more difficult issue as it is important to determine whether this is absence due to misconduct, for example time-keeping or being absent without leave, or whether this is due to sickness, for which the capability policy should be used. (The issue of sickness absence is dealt with in detail in *HR fundamentals: Employment Law*, to be published in May 2014).

The Employment Rights Act (1996) s1 puts an obligation on the employer to provide a statement of particulars, and in this should be included details of the discipline rules or where to find them. This ensures transparency and helps the employee understand that they are subject to these rules.

The concepts behind the process

Many Line Managers become concerned about the discipline procedure. They see it as a series of complicated steps that they need to follow and if they fail to take these convoluted steps they will face an Employment Tribunal. In fact the principles behind the process make it far easier to understand – it needs to be fair. To ensure that requirements for procedural justice are met:

- the process needs to be transparent and timely;
- those Managers that play a role should be trained;
- a thorough investigation must be carried out;
- employees need to have the time to prepare their case;
- employees should see any evidence against them, including witness statements;
- employees need the opportunity to have someone with them;
- if the employee or person accompanying them cannot attend, then it is reasonable to reconvene at another time;
- there should be a right to appeal.

As always there is a need to make some judgements over the extent of the above factors. For example Managers need some but not extensive training, investigation needs to determine the facts, but not be excessively long, and if the employee repeatedly cannot attend then it is reasonable for the meeting to be held in their absence. Employers need to make reasonable choices but to keep in mind the need for a fair procedure and a fair hearing.

The discipline process – misconduct

FIGURE 4.3   The discipline process adapted from ACAS (2011)

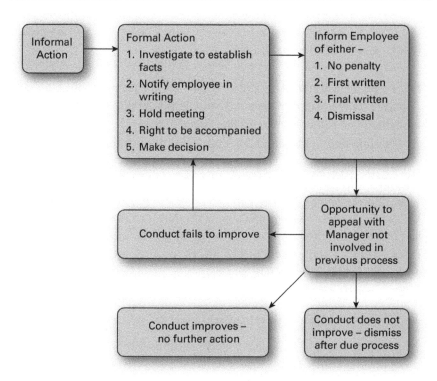

As we know, and the flowchart explains, the first step in a disciplinary is to deal with the issue informally. The employee may for example turn up late for work and may need a quick word to determine whether there is a problem that needs resolving, to prevent continuing lateness and ensure that the employee is fully aware of the employer's expectations. This informal word is important as it may be that, for example, the employee will tell the Line Manager of family or caring difficulties which may lead the Line Manager to suggest making different arrangements or to recommend that the employee makes a request for flexible working.

It is important that an informal conversation does not turn into formal action with, for example, set time limits for improvement. If the meeting has had a degree of formality an Employment Tribunal may view the meeting as a part of the formal process, and as such it is likely that the employee was not given the right to be accompanied. This happened in *London Underground v Ferenc-Batchelor* and *Harding v London Underground Ltd* (2003) ICR 656, EAT. Ms Ferenc-Batchelor drove her train through a red light and, though not given an oral warning, participated in a meeting which was adjourned for investigation. In her case the offence was sufficiently serious to go on to London Underground's formal discipline procedure. In the case of Mr Harding, who had repeated absence, he participated in a meeting and was given an oral warning, and notified in writing of this. For Mr Harding the informal warning remained on file for 12 months. Both of these cases were heard together by the EAT, which decided that these informal oral warnings were in fact part of the formal procedure and that London Underground Ltd had not given the two employees the right to be accompanied.

Though Line Managers have some discretion as to when the misconduct needs to be made formal, the HR professional should be aware that it is also important that there is a consistency in approach to misconduct throughout the organization and that rules are clear to all employees. If there are a variety of different practices it may be possible for employees to argue that they were unaware that the conduct was not allowed, or to question why others were allowed to do something that they are being disciplined for. The EAT argued for clarity of rules in the case of *Denco v Joinson* [1991] ICR 172, IRLR 63 when a Trade Union representative used another employee's password to gain access to parts of the company's system that he did not have access to. In this case the EAT stated that, despite the obvious nature of some rules, it would be sensible to state in writing that interfering with computers would carry serious consequences. Though the employee lost this case it remains wise to enforce a consistent and transparent approach to rules.

Making the misconduct discipline formal

Firstly it is important to note that the formal process provides for a number of warnings. ACAS suggests a three-step approach of first formal warning, written warning and dismissal (ACAS 2011), but the employer is free, within reason, to make its own choice on the number of stages.

Secondly the formal procedure can be accessed at any stage, and this is a matter of judgement for the Manager, with advice from the HR professional.

It may be that the employee's action is minimal but repeated and a first formal warning is appropriate. Alternatively the gravity of the employee's action, for example insubordination, warrants the process starting at a final written warning or even with the possible sanction of dismissal.

If after the informal warning the misconduct is repeated or a new misconduct occurs that warrants a formal approach then the employer should investigate to discover the facts. As always the HR professional will allocate a Manager with some experience of investigation, to the task and support them to investigate appropriately. Failure to carry out reasonable and impartial investigation will make any resulting dismissal unfair, *British Homes Stores v Burchell* (1980) ICR 303, EAT, and will also not have complied with the ACAS Code of Practice.

Once the investigation is completed, if disciplinary action is needed then the employee should be notified in writing and this is the responsibility of the HR professional. The letter will state what is alleged, the possible consequences of the action, and give enough information for the employee to prepare their case. The employee will be given information on the venue and time of the meeting and will be reminded of the right to be accompanied by a colleague or Trade Union representative.

To prepare their case fully they will need to know the full allegations made against them, for example in *Hotson v Wishbech Conservative Club* (1984) ICT 859 EAT, the employee, a barmaid, was said to have been accused of inefficiency in managing bar takings when in fact she was accused of dishonesty. She was unable to dispute the allegation of dishonesty as she thought she was being accused of inefficiency. When dismissed she claimed and won her case of unfair dismissal.

The meeting

The HR professional will have advised management on who could carry out the meeting but the Manager taking the discipline meeting will, if possible, be different to the one that carried out the investigation. Prior to the meeting the Manager holding the disciplinary will have read through the investigation report, any attached evidence and read any papers that the employee has presented. Thought should have been given as to whether the employee or their companion needs any reasonable adjustments to normal proceeding, such as an interpreter or ground floor access. The HR professional will be responsible for taking notes during the meeting and advising the Manager during the decision-making.

During the meeting the Manager will discuss the allegation, giving the employee the opportunity to state their case. The Code of Practice explains that the following steps should be followed during the meeting:

- The employer should explain the allegation and go through the evidence.
- The employee should be allowed to reply and answer allegations.
- The employee and employer may ask questions, present evidence or may question evidence from witnesses statements.
- The employee may call witnesses but the employer needs advance notice of any witnesses that will attend.
- The discussion then is summed up before the employer adjourns to make a decision.

Whilst the decision depends on the facts, the level of sanction is a matter of judgement. The following need to be taken into account:

- the circumstance of the situation;
- the sanction given for similar action in the past;
- any current warnings;
- the reasonableness of any sanction given.

Following the meeting the HR professional will send the employee a letter informing them of the decision and this will include the nature of the misconduct, the change in behaviour required, the right of appeal and the fact that a further offence may result in further sanctions. If the sanction is a warning then this will remain on file for a defined number of months and will cease to be live once this period has passed. The case law on expired warning leads HR professionals to err on the side of caution and disregard spent warnings, *Airbus UK Ltd v Webb*, Court of Appeal, (2008) EWCA Civ 49 and *Diosynth Ltd v Thomson*, Court of Session (Inner House), (2006) IRLR 284.

The appeal

If an employee requests an appeal, it should be held as soon as is reasonable by a Manager who has not been involved in the previous hearings. If any additional evidence has come to light then the case should be reheard, with all the evidence being reviewed. Alternatively the Manager will need to review the process to ensure that it was carried out fairly. Whatever the approach employees should inform the employer of the grounds for the appeal so that this can be investigated further. Grounds may include additional evidence but also the harshness of the sanction, procedural unfairness or lack of impartiality of the disciplining Manager. The Manager will prepare for the meeting in detail as before. The situation may be more complex with the further information provided, or may be focused on one area, depending on the grounds of the appeal.

Few employees go through a discipline meeting and even fewer an appeal meeting, and it is important that the Manager explain the purpose of the meeting to the employee, along with the process it will take, the scope of the meeting and any subsequent decisions. Apart from this the meeting, decision and letter are very similar to that of the discipline meeting.

Gross misconduct

Whilst Managers may feel more comfortable having had experience of discipline meetings, even competent Managers may not feel comfortable dealing with gross misconduct issues, unless the situation is very clear. They know that mistakes over gross misconduct may lead them to an Employment Tribunal. Examples of actions of gross misconduct will have been listed in the discipline procedure.

Gross misconduct should be dealt with in the same fair and equitable manner as other discipline meetings and decisions. Employment Tribunals, when determining unfair dismissal claims, use the case of *British Home Stores v Burchell* (1980) ICR 303, EAT, in which the EAT made some helpful statements. This case states that the employer needs to ensure that they have a genuine belief, based on reasonable grounds after reasonable investigation, that the employee did carry out the alleged action. This means that adequate investigation must be carried out, and it may be necessary to suspend the employee – either for the safety of the accused employee, for the security of witnesses or to prevent any further action. The reason for dismissal must be clear to the employer and employee and not a pretext and that when looking at the evidence available to the disciplining Manager, there are reasonable grounds for believing that the employee did carry out the misconduct.

The discipline process – poor performance

The first step is to determine whether the poor performance is due to laziness and deliberate lack of willingness or a real inability to complete the task to the standard required. This is an important judgement as it is as wrong to take a struggling employee and discipline them for laziness as it is to take a lazy employee and provide them with training. One makes a possibly loyal but weak employee resentful and the other undermines the authority of the Manager. The HR professional could act as a useful tool here to support the Line Manager to determine which of the two approaches should be taken and it may be that investigation of the situation may provide evidence that will advise their decision.

Once it is decided that it is truly an issue of poor performance and a thorough investigation has been carried out, then a letter will be composed by the HR professional providing details of the poor performance, what the possible sanction might be, that they will have the opportunity to state their case and that they have the right to be accompanied by a colleague or Trade Union representative. The meeting will be held in the same manner as with the discipline meeting but it is the actions following the decision in which capacity differs from conduct. The HR professional will inform the employee of the decision in writing, as an 'improvement note' which details:

- the performance problem;
- the improvement that is required;
- the timescale this improvement should be achieved in;
- the support that will be offered;
- the review date.

In this case it is imperative that the support agreed between employee and employer takes place as agreed. Without adequate support it would render any further action, including dismissal, unfair. It may be that the employee, without the appropriate training, cannot achieve the standard required and so impacts negatively on the business performance. They cannot legally be dismissed until the support required has been given. If the training is given and despite all reasonable support the employee still is unable to achieve the required standard, then it may be necessary to take further action.

One final thought that should be considered in the process of managing poor performance is any issue of disability. It may be that the standard is not being reached because adequate assistance has not been given to someone with a disability. It may be by changing the process in small ways, by using special aids and adaptations, by supporting others in the team in their understanding of disability, that the employee may be able to reach the standard required.

The checklist below provides some direction for HR professionals preparing a discipline procedure. In this case conduct and capability (poor performance) are covered together.

The case study on page 112 gives three examples of cases of capability which can help us to see how we could improve our own practice.

TABLE 4.1   Checklist for a Discipline Procedure

1. Is the Discipline Procedure in writing?	Yes/No
2. Have employees been given the Discipline Procedure or been notified of where it can be found?	Yes/No
3. Is there access to policies that mention what is expected on timekeeping, absence, alcohol and drug use, conduct, telephone and internet use?	Yes/No
4. Does the policy explain that all issues will be investigated and that no discipline will be carried out until it has been fully investigated?	Yes/No
5. Does it detail examples of gross misconduct?	Yes/No
6. Does the policy state that employees will be invited in writing to a meeting and that the letter will explain: • what is alleged; • what the possible sanction might be; • that they will have the opportunity to state their case; • that they have the right to be accompanied by a colleague or Trade Union representative?	Yes/No
7. Does it give details of the first warning and final written warning?	Yes/No
8. Does the policy explain that warnings will be in writing?	Yes/No

TABLE 4.1 *continued*

9. For conduct, does it explain that warnings will give details of: • the nature of the misconduct; • the change in behaviour required; • the right of appeal; • the fact that a further offence may result in a written warning?	Yes/No
10. For performance, does it explain that warnings will give details of • the problem; • the standard of performance required; • the timescale; • any help that will be given?	Yes/No
11. Does the policy explain the length of time the warning will be on record?	Yes/No
12. Does it explain that the dismissal meeting will be held by a senior Manager?	Yes/No
13. Does it explain that if dismissal is upheld the employee will be notified in writing?	Yes/No
14. For dismissal, does the policy make it clear that the letter will explain: • the reason for the dismissal; • the date that employment will be terminated; • the right of appeal?	Yes/No
15. Does the policy give a time limit for appealing a decision?	Yes/No
16. Does it state that a senior Manager will hear the appeal and that the decision is final?	Yes/No
17. Does the policy explain that for gross misconduct the employee may be suspended on full pay whilst an investigation is carried out?	Yes/No
18. Does it explain that if dismissed for gross misconduct they will be informed in writing that they are to be summarily dismissed without notice or payment in lieu of notice?	Yes/No

CASE STUDY   Employment Law on poor performance

With the removal of the Default Retirement Age in the UK the use of capability as a means to dismissal may increase. The following cases will look at some particular issues surrounding capability.

The first case stresses the need to give the employee the opportunity to improve. In many cases Line Managers, when they decide to make the issue formal, want a swift process. However, justice requires the opportunity to improve. In *Mansfield Hosiery Mills Ltd v Bromley* EAT (1977) IRLR 301, a precedent-setting case, the claimant was a boiler service fitter and though the job advertisement had stated that training would be given, it wasn't. He did well and was promoted but when there were complaints about his lack of enthusiasm he was warned once orally and once in writing. Eventually things came to a head and he was dismissed. The claimant won the case because he was not given the opportunity to improve – the employer should have given the employee a clear explanation of the standard he needed to reach, what behaviour constituted improvement and the timescale for this improvement.

The case of *Davidson v Kent Meters Ltd* (1975) IRLR 145 reinforces this in that the case enforces the requirement to warn employees of the need for improvement. In this case an assembler fitted 471 faulty parts out of 500 but was not warned in writing that their job was at risk (or given the right to appeal). This shows that it is a fair procedure that is important; in this case the fitter claimed that her supervisor had instructed her wrongly.

The final case refers to an unusual situation where poor performance becomes apparent over time. In *Miller v Executor of John C Graham* (1978) IRLR 309, it was shown that a series of insignificant incidents may demonstrate that an employee is not capable of conducting their job. The claimant was a farm manager, and after a number of small incidents he was given a warning. He improved, but after further deterioration he was dismissed. He failed at his claim for unfair dismissal, with the case showing that even a series of unimportant failings in performance might result in the need for significant intervention, requiring dismissal if no improvement is made. However, an employee must be given the opportunity to improve.

Conflict – collective dispute resolution

We as HR Professionals will be familiar with advising Line Managers in discipline and grievance. Fewer HR Managers have experience of collective dispute resolution. This makes the knowledge and skills particularly valuable for those employing Employee Relations specialists. We will look at the practice of collective bargaining and negotiation, through to industrial action.

Collective bargaining

Collective bargaining is the use of a collective body, the Trade Union, to negotiate over certain terms and conditions. The TULR(C) Act (1992) s178 (2) initially described the range of terms and conditions that can be consulted upon but this was extended by the Employment Relations Act (1999) to cover what is agreed by the parties. Unions can, for example, bargain or negotiate about basic pay rates, overtime payments, hours of work, access to training or holiday entitlement.

Practical Considerations

FIGURE 4.4   The process of Union recognition

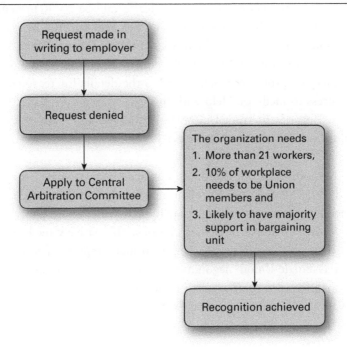

The first step for the Union is for it to be recognized by the employer. The Union may apply to the employer (through the HR department). If this request is accepted by the company then there are no further processes to go through and the Union can bargain with the employer. If the employer declines to recognize the Union then it may apply to the Central Arbitration Committee. The process of recognition is shown in Figure 4.4.

Often there is disagreement between the employer and the Union concerning the scope of the bargaining unit (ie the group of employees that the Union will negotiate for). The bargaining unit extends further than just the Union members, as it may include for example all the employees in a particular profession or at a particular grade. It benefits the Union to have smaller bargaining units, so that issues are clear but employers prefer larger bargaining units, so that they can ensure they meet equal pay legislation, can harmonize terms and conditions and are not endlessly negotiating with different bargaining units. Disputes can be resolved through the Central Arbitration Committee.

In practice at each site there will be an elected Trade Union Representative who is given paid time off to carry out their Trade Union duties and to be trained. These duties include members' meetings, accompanying members at grievance and discipline meetings, and collective bargaining. There are other types of representatives, such as Health and Safety Representatives and Union Learning Representatives who are also covered by the Trade Union Labour Relations (Consolidation) Act (1992) for time off to complete their duties and training. Often employers working with Unions establish an agreement or protocol which identifies the details for reasonable time off and access to facilities. Help with this can be found in ACAS' Code of Practice 3: Time off for Trade Union Duties and Activities (2010) and Trade Union Representation in the Workplace (2009d).

If there is more than one Union recognized by a company, the Unions will need to decide how the representations to the company will be made. It may be that the Unions will negotiate directly with the company, in which case it is known as 'Single Table' negotiations. Alternatively, the Unions may meet together and decide on one Union to make representations and this is known as 'Single Union' negotiations. Single Union negotiations may be more straightforward for the parties and often there is agreement not to resort to industrial action prematurely.

For collective bargaining purposes Trade Unions will need specific information from the employer. This will ensure that the process of collective bargaining is fair, with the Trade Union having access to information that will substantiate their claim. However the employer is also able to withhold certain information which, for example, may be sensitive to their competitiveness and cause substantial injury to the employer if it was released. Any disputes over access to information are dealt with through the Central Arbitration Committee and further details can be found in the ACAS (2003) Code of Practice 2: Disclosure of Information to Trade Unions for Collective Bargaining Purposes.

Bargaining

The Union may bargain at single-site or corporate level, multi-employer level, industry level or national level. It is the employer that chooses at what level to bargain, but in many companies it is at decentralized corporate level that bargaining takes place. This gives the employer bargaining leverage – to understand the reason behind this we need to briefly look at demand and supply.

In a non-unionized company as demand for labour increases the level of wages increase, especially for professional skills. In recessionary times, when there are more available unemployed workers – whilst it is difficult to reduce the level of wages there may be less overtime available, entry level wages may be less. This also enables companies to make essential cost savings but any differences between wages in the workforce may need to be justified in order to protect against an equal pay claim.

In unionized organizations as demand for labour increases the wages increase. However, in recessionary times the fixed wage agreement makes it more difficult for companies to reduce their salary costs. The company reduces its costs and manages any reduction in workload by making redundancies. However, in the recession of 2007–08 in the UK redundancies were avoided by reducing working hours.

If the company bargains directly with the Union at a corporate level then any wage increases made may be passed to the consumer as the employer may not be able to absorb these extra costs. There is a risk that the higher price of products may reduce the number of consumers as they switch to a competitor's lower priced product. The company may therefore find that they can make an argument for wage constraint to protect jobs.

Industrial action

If negotiations fail then the Union may choose to take action such as an overtime ban, rest-day working ban or strike. It is only possible here to give an introduction of the core elements of what is complex law, but it may be pertinent to mention here that whilst an overtime ban and strike will be legal if procedure is followed, a work-to-rule, where an employee does not complete all contractual tasks, will not be legal.

Firstly in the UK there is no legal right to strike – the natural consequence of this would be that when striking a Union member would have breached their employment contract, and could be disciplined. However the law has allowed for Union action to be immune if the action 'was taken in contemplation or furtherance of an industrial dispute' s219, TULR(C) Act (1992). This is known as the 'golden formula'. Immunity is lost and the strike becomes unlawful in a number of cases, but particularly if there is no valid ballot, if there is unlawful secondary action or unlawful picketing.

The procedures for balloting are intricate and it is not necessary to identify them here. However we do need to identify what an employer should expect:

- The Union will start by notifying the employer of the ballot, including a sample voting paper. Specific details of what should be included in the notice are found in s226A, TULR (C) Act (1992).

- As soon as reasonably possible after the ballot the employer should be informed of the results of the ballot by the Union, s231A, TULR (C) Act (1992).

- The employer will receive notice of industrial action from the Union, and this will be received at least by the seventh day before the strike, s234A, TULR (C) Act (1992). In this notification the employer should be told whether this will be continuous industrial action or a set period of strike action, in which case the dates should be given. The Union will also identify the affected employees so that the employer is aware of who may be on strike on the dates given.

- More details can be found in the Code of Practice: Industrial Action Ballots and Notice to Employers (BIS, 2005).

During the strike it is not lawful for employers to recruit temporary employees to cover for employees that are on strike, s7 (1a), The Conduct of Employment Agencies and Employment Business Regulations (2003), though they can use employees employed directly to cover and any temporary staff already in the business to do work but not to cover directly. It is not lawful for the employer to dismiss the strikers whilst taking official industrial action, s238, TULR(C) Act (1992) – however, an employer may choose not to pay employees whilst they are on strike, s14 (5), Employment Rights Act (1996). When the employee returns to work the period of strike action does not count towards their length of service but they retain continuous service s216, Employment Rights Act (1996).

For the Union during the strike, those employees taking part in the dispute may picket. This means that employees may attend at or near their workplace to peacefully communicate information or persuade others to join the strike. s220, TULR(C) Act (1992), gives the 'right' to picket within the law. The Picketing Code of Practice (BIS, 1992) provides details of the implications of civil law on picketing.

The case study below provides two examples of cases of strikes and picketing which have informed practice.

CASE STUDY Employment Law and action short of industrial action

The focus has been on the involvement of the employer in collective bargaining, and what the employer should expect in the event of a strike. Taking a similar approach the following cases look at practical issues about industrial action short of strike action and picketing.

In the case of *Midland Plastics v Till and ors* (1983) ICR 118, EAT a member of the works committee threatened industrial action by 11am on 5 May. However they were dismissed before the deadline and all claimed unfair dismissal. The Tribunal agreed with the employer that they were not yet taking industrial action and that threats were the last stage of a negotiation process. However in making the judgement the kinds of activity that could be seen as industrial action short of a strike were identified – go-slows, overtime ban, working to rule and picketing.

In *Gate Gourmet London Ltd v Transport and General Workers' Union and ors* (2005) IRLR 881, QBD the issue of intimidating picketing was taken up. Gate Gourmet London was in the process of attempting to make changes to ensure its financial security when unofficial action led to 622 employees being dismissed. The dismissed employees picketed outside two sites with pickets from six to 200 people at different locations. Gate Gourmet London Ltd sought to reduce the pickets to no more than 10. In consideration of the request, Mr Justice Fulford had regard to Article 11 of the European Convention of Human Rights and the UK history of democratic opposition. However he restricted the activity and numbers of pickets at the sites, with no more than six as suggested by the Code of Practice (BIS, 1992).

Conclusion

The mechanisms of discipline and grievance are foremost tools for ensuring that both parties meet their obligations, and the HR professional has the responsibility to ensure that the approach is both legal and fair. With employers that recognize Unions, the HR professional will endeavour to build an effective working relationship with the Union and will meet its obligations so that bargaining can take place. If industrial action takes place the HR professional will advise Line Managers on how to manage those continuing work and those that are picketing. Communication is fundamental throughout all Employee Relations and the case study below discusses the challenge of giving bad news to employees.

The next chapter puts this together by looking at the planning and action required for EIP and individual and collective dispute resolution.

CASE STUDY   Communicating bad news

Redundancy is addressed in detail in *HR Fundamentals: Employment Law*, published in May 2014, but redundancy communication is mentioned here as it can be a complex and delicate task.

The HR Department needs to ensure that any discussions about redundancies are restricted so that those who will be at risk of redundancy do not hear from unofficial channels. Those that will need to be told include the Trade Union, employees that will be at risk of redundancy and those remaining after the redundancies. Managers of the teams affected will be informed as they may well be meeting the employees at risk of redundancy.

Trade Unions will require information in order to make consultation meaningful. The Line Manager, supported by the HR professional, will inform those at risk of redundancy. An understanding of the needs of employees receiving bad news will help the HR professional in ensuring a private environment, a brief and consistent message, and a reassurance that there is some support available. Employees may be upset or angry, shocked and uncertain how they will manage and will need time to assimilate the message before they have questions. Finally those that are not being made redundant will also need time and it is necessary to have an understanding of their needs while social bonds are being wrenched apart. They may also be angry, or feel guilty that they were not made redundant. They may also feel that they might be next. They need reassurance that the company is acting legally and that their jobs are safe.

For each of these audiences different media will be chosen. It may be appropriate to meet with the whole company to communicate the reason for the redundancies, a formal meeting will be held with Trade Unions representatives and affected employees will be seen individually. It may be that those not affected still need to meet with their Line Manager individually for reassurance.

The questionnaire overleaf helps the HR professional to evaluate the organization's communication mechanisms.

DIAGNOSTIC QUESTIONNAIRE Communication

	Yes	No
1 When there is downward communication to give do you identify the audience?	☐	☐
2 Do you make sure the message is consistent?	☐	☐
3 Do you think about communication throughout the employee lifecycle?	☐	☐
4 Do you provide opportunities for employees to formally discuss processes and the best ways of working?	☐	☐
5 Do you recognize employees who pass on good practice?	☐	☐
6 Do you provide opportunities for employees to contribute to decision-making?	☐	☐
7 Do you have formal processes for listening to employees?	☐	☐
8 Do you encourage and train Managers to listen in all circumstances, including grievance and discipline?	☐	☐
9 Do you have an organizational culture that promotes open communication?	☐	☐

Scores

Questions 1–3 relate to downward communication, questions 4–6 relate to lateral communication and questions 7–9 relate to employee voice.

Between 9 and 7 positive answers

At 9 positive answers your organization is able to communicate effectively, planning communications within the organization to keep messages consistent. It will also effectively encourage employees to pass on good practice and will encourage Line Managers to listen effectively. At 7 positive answers your organization will be very good at one aspect of communication and have an approach to its employees which values their contribution.

Between 6 and 5 positive answers

Your organization has some idea of how to communicate, value your teams' contributions and listen to employees. Dependent on the distribution of answers, at 6 positive answers your organization will usually be reasonable at downward communication. It is usually the approach of individual Managers that reduces the scores.

Between 4 and 2 positive answers

Your organization has not focused on the power of communication or its role in improving employee relations. Depending on the distribution of questions there may be one area that the organization has some prior experience in – usually downward communication. There is much that you can do to improve communication in your organization.

Planning and action

05

This section looks at the planning and skills needed for the main areas of Employee Relations – Employee Involvement and Participation, and Individual and Collective Dispute Resolution. We review how EIP can be managed and the issues involved in implementing schemes taking two examples, partnership working and quality circles. In previous chapters we have touched on the need for Dispute Resolution methods that can resolve issues early and here we take a very practical view of planning the process of Mediation. In the previous chapter we discussed collective bargaining; the third area that we look at is how to plan and carry out a negotiation.

The CIPD has identified a number of different behaviours that all HR professionals should exhibit and has identified these as part of the HR professions map (CIPD, 2012e). The behaviours include the ability to be a skilled influencer, a decisive thinker, be curious and work collaboratively. These align closely to the skills discussed throughout the chapter – investigating, influencing, active listening and team-work.

In this chapter we will discuss:

- how to design and implement effective EIP schemes;
- how to ensure that Mediation or EIP schemes are successful;
- how to prepare for and carry out a grievance meeting;
- the skills needed to carry out investigations;
- how to carry out interviews and listen actively;
- how to develop a Mediation scheme;
- how to prepare for collective bargaining and negotiation;
- how to minimize the effects of industrial action on the employer.

Involvement and participation

As mentioned in Chapter 3, the choice of an EIP scheme is dependent on the business strategy. It is also dependent on the organization's history, social attitudes and legislation. We will take two EIP methods, Partnership working and Quality Circles, and evaluate what makes these effective in organizations.

Partnership working

One particular type of EIP method, which is relevant in today's unionized organizations, is partnership working. Partnership working is when the employer and the Trade Union (or any other collective representation of employees such as a works council or forum) work closely together. In order for this to be effective, both parties must have similar values and aims. These have been identified by the TUC and Luckhurst and Jameson (2011) as being:

- joint commitment to the organization's success;
- recognition of the legitimate interests of each party;
- joint commitment to employment security;
- joint focus on the quality of working life;
- joint commitment to operating in a transparent manner;
- joint commitment to add value to the arrangement.

It involves mutual trust, respecting the different approaches and interests of each party and mutual interest in the organization's success.

In order for partnership to work effectively the senior management and Union representatives should all fully support it. It is often useful for senior management to drive the project initially and to hold preliminary discussions with the Union. This supports both parties as they form a view as to what this partnership will be like and determine the scope of consultation. Once a common understanding has been reached then the senior managers may then pass the job of establishing an agreement to a steering committee, though with regular updates. It is the steering committee which will prepare the written agreement.

The written agreement will clarify the practicalities of the partnership. These may include:

- the number and frequency of meetings;
- the scope of consultation;
- the form of consultation;
- how employees will be communicated with after the meeting;
- a code of conduct;
- how any disagreements will be managed;
- details for terminating the partnership, in the event that one or both parties wishes to end the agreement.

Once the agreement has formally been achieved there are two ways that employees may be informed. In some organizations the partnership is communicated by face-to-face meetings and this gives the opportunity for both parties to be seen to support this together. It is good practice for Union members to vote on the partnership agreement, and the Union therefore may wish to convince its members of the value of the agreement. For all parties that will be involved in the partnership training is vital, both to pass on the details of the agreement but also to prepare them for the process. Luckhurst and Jameson (2011) suggest independent training and provide a list of possible skills gaps for training, which includes:

- understanding the link between partnership and engagement;
- negotiation;
- developing the code of conduct;
- asking strategic questions;
- understanding partnership behaviour and tactics;
- disseminating and embedding partnership working.

It is important that both parties are aware of the process of consultation. One approach that can be used is option-based consultation. The reasons for a business objective and its impact on employees and the organization, are discussed and the partnership members given a number of options. In organizations without a partnership agreement this decision would be made by the Board or senior directors, but with a partnership agreement the options are discussed fully, in confidence, with employee representatives. The employee representatives may also bring alternative options to discuss.

Management have the final decision, and as with any decision not all participants will agree with the final decision, but they have had a real opportunity to influence it. Once the option has been chosen, then the meeting also has the opportunity to discuss how that decision will be communicated to employees and any other issues that are involved, depending on the decision made.

If the Union does not feel that they have a real opportunity to influence decision-making then this will impact on the trust between the Union and the employer, and the partnership will be threatened. So it is in the interest of both parties that the discussions are effective.

The case study below gives a very short illustration of how UNISON worked with Bristol City Council Libraries to improve the working life of librarians.

CASE STUDY   Bristol City Council libraries

The Bristol City Council Libraries had been subject to some restructuring and redundancies which meant, in practice, that librarians found themselves being moved from library to library with very little notice. This impacted on librarians' life outside work, and though some of the changes had been positive the morale of the librarians was low. An initial consultation carried out by the Council showed that there was some demand for change, and in particular some interest in Sunday opening. The Council proposed a pilot with the following aims:

- to introduce more flexible working and Sunday opening;

- to introduce partnership working;

- to produce better work-life balance;

- to achieve more flexible service delivery;

- to produce benefits for both employees and the Council.

The librarians initially were unenthusiastic but UNISON felt there was some worth to the project and encouraged employees to get involved.

A set of ground rules were agreed, and then both parties went about investigating the possibly of improving flexible working and Sunday opening. Two surveys were sent out, one with pay and conditions for Sunday working, to establish interest. The second survey gave options for different ways of managing flexible working, such as compressed hours or flexitime, and sufficient numbers of librarians were interested for the Council to establish a focus group.

Self-managed rotas were set up which helped librarians manage their life outside work and the involvement in this helped improve morale. This freed up time for managers who often had to deal with rotas or complaints about rotas. Sunday opening was developed with the support of librarians, despite the initial resistance.

(Adapted from Bristol City Council: Times of Our Lives Project, TUC: 2001)

Quality Circles

Establishing effective employee participation has been a particularly difficult task in the UK and quality circles are a good example of this. Quality Circles consist of groups of employees without the involvement of management, who meet regularly to analyze work processes and to improve these practices. However the individualistic nature of employees has meant that, whilst quality circles have flourished in Japan, where the culture is collective and loyalty to the business is strong, quality circles have been more difficult to implement effectively in the UK.

The approach taken in the UK in recent years has been to focus on employee engagement. The single most effective driver for engagement has been the ability to give upward feedback of views (CIPD, 2012f). The methods that can provide the opportunity for this include Suggestion Schemes, Employee Works Councils, Quality Circles or Employee Forums. Whichever voice mechanisms are chosen, the following circumstances need to be encouraged (IPA and Tomorrow's Company, 2012):

- safety to speak;
- an atmosphere of trust;
- participative leadership style;
- voice is valued, and the process is authentic;
- an inclusive culture;
- devolvement of responsibility;

- training for Managers to encourage voice;
- a range of formal channels for voice.

Conflict – individual dispute resolution

We can add value to the business if we have the skills to support Line Managers in their management of grievances, and we therefore spend some time evaluating the skills required for grievance handling and we focus also on the skills needed to support mediation.

The skills for effective grievance handling

Grievance handing is often a concern to new HR professionals. Managing grievances can be challenging, as they may involve difficult conversations and at times high emotions. We are aware that we need to use our judgement and apply our own knowledge of employment law so as to solve the problem and protect the employer from Employment Tribunal claims.

Carrying out a grievance meeting

In some cases the grievance letter has provided enough information for investigation to be carried out prior to the meeting. In most situations the grievance meeting is carried out prior to investigation, because the employee making the grievance needs to be heard and some grievances can be complex. Also any consequences of making a formal grievance need to be discussed. All of these factors dictate the timing of the grievance meeting.

The grievance meeting should be held in a private office and the meeting led by an impartial Manager who will have prepared by reading the letter. Notes will need to be taken, particularly if the grievance is complex, to assist the investigating manager.

Active listening

Though this seems fairly basic it is where most Managers fail. Often we may start by listening effectively but our other responsibilities distract us from listening further. This is the reason why we need to practise listening – it is a skill that demands concentration and needs a deliberate effort. We need to:

- Pay continual attention to the employee and what is being said. It is important also to observe body language as this gives a clue to the feelings of the employee who may be upset.

- Encourage the employee to continue explaining; this can be done by showing them we are listening, by nodding or occasionally saying 'yes', which gives them the opportunity to continue.

- Ask questions to clarify points and ask for further details.

- Summarize what is being explained so that both parties know what has been understood.

Record keeping

At all interviews written records should be taken. The investigation manager may make some notes during interviews with witnesses but at the grievance meeting itself we are often the person tasked with this. Where possible the records should be verbatim. This is easier for witness testimonies, which is why the investigation manager may make these notes, but it is harder in grievance meetings, where there may be strong feelings and the pace of the meeting may be fast. If necessary the note-taker must ask for time to record conversations or ask for comments to be repeated – all parties want the records to be accurate. In some companies a digital recorder may be acceptable but it continues to be rarely used, and written evidence is required for an Employment Tribunal.

Carrying out investigations

An investigation is the examination of the facts of a workplace incident, and the search for evidence to substantiate these facts in order to influence a decision. Investigations are a necessary part of grievance and discipline procedures in order that a just and fair decision is made. However it is important that we note that a workplace investigation is an internal investigation which does not need the extent of skills and process required for a police investigation. One of the main challenges when arranging for a manager to carry out an investigation is finding the balance that an HR professional needs to give to their initial explanation of the task. We need to ensure that the manager will take the task on with an appreciation of the gravity and responsibility involved but that the manager also realizes that this is a workplace and not a criminal investigation. Evidence is required to identify what has happened and so make a decision which is well-founded on the balance of probabilities and not by a proof of guilt.

Ideally, investigations should be carried out by trained and impartial managers, who are not the Line Manager of the employee making the grievance or any employee associated with the grievance. The HR professional will usually not carry out the investigation themselves but will manage the process, supporting the investigating manager and ensuring that the process is carried out fairly and within reasonable time limits.

Investigating managers may need support in preparing a robust investigation plan. This is an identification of the evidence to be gathered, whether by the interviewing of witnesses or documentary evidence. There is a range of documentary evidence that may help the investigation and these may include reports, policies or personnel records, hard drives, emails or voice recordings. The evidence that could assist depends on the actual grievance itself but, for example, if the grievance concerns the attendance or location of employees then gathering evidence may involve accessing attendance software, CCTV footage or hard-copy diaries or calendars. Managers may need support to understand what sources of information are available in a particular organization, but well-trained investigation managers will have learnt to ask for a range of sources of information rather than taking what they are given by the HR professional.

Investigation managers will need to logically and systematically plan the investigation. Some evidence may deteriorate – for example, witness memories will fade, documentation may get lost or CCTV tapes reused. There may be the need to interview some witnesses first to get an initial idea of the facts, which may then be substantiated or contradicted by other witness statements. However, the plan will need to have flexibility so that witnesses can be re-interviewed if further evidence comes to light.

Finally we will act as case manager to ensure that the investigation is completed within reasonable time limits and that the evidence, and often a report by the investigation manager, is received and stored safely.

Witnesses

Guidance on dealing with witnesses wishing to remain anonymous has been given in the case of *Linfood Cash and Carry Ltd v Thomson and anor* (1989) ICR 518. The action of the employer in managing the need for anonymity will involve the attempt to balance the need for the employee to have a fair hearing and ensuring the safety of witnesses. The case recommends that employers:

- Reduce the information in the written witness statement to preserve anonymity.
- Note the date, time and place of the incident or observation, the witness's opportunity to observe clearly and any circumstantial evidence, such as knowledge of a system, reason for the witness's presence, memorable small data or whether the witness has any reason to fabricate their evidence.
- Aim to support the witness statement with corroborating evidence.
- Should make the written statement of the witness available to the employee and their representatives.

Interviewing

The main tool the investigating manager will use is questioning. When interviewing witnesses questions are used to:

- gather information;
- explore feelings, attitudes and observe responses;
- stimulate discussion or help the witness think through something; and
- clarify an issue.

The investigating manager will have planned a logical sequence to the questions but will start with an introductory statement explaining the circumstances leading to the interview, confirming that notes will be taken, and how they may be used. Questions to encourage the witness to talk need to be open, where to determine facts questions may be closed. Probing questions gain more detailed answers and clarify facts. Questioning may gather corroborating evidence and will distinguish between first-hand and second-hand evidence. It is important during the interview to use questions to determine between facts and interpretations. At the end of the interview the investigating manager will check contact details, will explain when and how the notes will be sent for confirmation of accuracy and when the investigation is thought to be finished. The witnesses will need to know that they are to keep their involvement in the process confidential. They also need to know that there may be a possibility that they may be asked to go to an Employment Tribunal.

It might be that the investigating manager may need to return to check details or corroborate evidence. The investigating manager should not spend too long before completing the investigation.

Decisions

Whether there is substance to the grievance or not the Manager will need to meet again with the employee to agree the outcome. Where the grievance is real, the employee may be able to achieve the action they originally desired, but for others that may not be possible. Often procedures impact on business or on other employees, which means that it is not possible to resolve the grievance in the way that is wished and some compromise may need to be made.

Though the issues and legislation surrounding harassment or bullying is outside the scope of this book, it is important to recognize the duty of care an employer has and if a grievance concerning this has been received, there is no compromise to be made. Employees that have been subject to bullying or harassment should be protected and the employer should have a separate policy to deal with such situations.

The scenario below describes a typical situation in a small business with two problems with employees.

Scenario

Courthands Ltd

Courthands Ltd was a supplier of building and plumbing materials and equipment to the construction trade, with five merchant yards throughout the South East and a small number of employees at each site. The HR Department in Bracknell was also very small, with two HR professionals who both travelled to sites to support Line Managers and manage any issues. Caroline had been called to support the Manager of the Camberley site where there were two grievances.

Firstly, the Manager telephoned Caroline to inform her that one of the employees, Charlie, had not received the correct Christmas bonus in his December pay, and that some of his pay had been deducted from his wages for a pension that he had not agreed to. Even though there was no letter she accepted that there was a grievance to deal with. Caroline checked with payroll, who confirmed that Charlie had not opted out of the pension and that the Manager had only confirmed the Christmas bonus after the deadline for the December payroll. She discussed the options that payroll had for

▶

making the bonus payment. Caroline explained to the Manager what she had found from payroll and they agreed to meet with Charlie together.

She used a private office that the Manager had arranged for her to meet with Charlie. He was rather irritated that the company had not paid him his money, particularly as it was just after the Christmas period and money was short. She proposed to deal with the bonus payment first and the Manager explained his mistake. Caroline went on to describe the options that were available and agreed, after discussions with payroll, to make sure the payment was in Charlie's bank account by Friday. She then proceeded to explain what had happened about the pension. When she checked that Charlie had received notification about the pension, she was able to explain that Charlie should not have thrown the paperwork away, but that he could opt out if he had wished by sending in the slip at the bottom of the form. She had brought another form with her and Charlie completed it so that Caroline could pass it to payroll back in Bracknell.

Caroline then moved on to deal with the second grievance, which had been received in a letter to her five days previously and was a more serious issue. She had arranged to meet with the employee, Jake.

Apparently Jake was one of a few young men who had joined a team whose members had worked for the company for many years. He had found settling in quite difficult, particularly as some of the team continuously made homophobic comments to Jake and excluded him from their conversations. Jake felt comfortable enough with Caroline to explain that he was gay. Jake had also seen the team laughing and joking with the Manager and although they did not use unacceptable language when the Manager was with them, Jake felt that the Manager would not do anything to help him.

Caroline suggested that Jake did talk to the Manager, but suggested that she had a quick word as well. She believed that his feelings that he wouldn't be supported by the Manager were an important part of the issue. She recorded this in her notes, along with a reminder to check with both the Manager and Jake later in the month to see if the situation had improved, and to check whether the Manager had attended any discrimination training recently.

Caroline discussed the issue with the Manager who had not been aware of any problem. Caroline agreed to monitor the situation but she had to take care not to undermine the Manager and to maintain the trust that she had

◄

built up with the Manager over the years. The Manager had made a mistake with the bonus and he also seemed very close to the old team, doing little to support new members and not realizing that there was a serious problem – he would need to visit Camberley a little more often in the future.

Mediation

Choosing an approach

Firstly we might remind ourselves of the benefits of mediation and the issues that are suitable for mediation. In the United States mediation is already well established but is less so in the UK, although it has gained prominence with the Gibbons Review (2007). Mediation at its best can support Line Managers in the management of their teams and can have a positive impact on organizational culture, particularly as it reflects a pluralist approach and the value of the employee. Some of the benefits of using mediation are listed below:

TABLE 5.1   Benefits of using mediation as a means of resolving workplace issues, adapted from Latreille (2010: 6)

Benefits of using mediation as a means of resolving workplace issues	%
To retain valuable employees	62.8
To reduce sick absence	32.8
To develop a culture of managing & developing people	54.3
To improve relationships between employees	83.3
To avoid costs in defending ET claims	47.9
To maintain confidentiality	18.9
To reduce/eliminate stress of more formal processes	70.7
To reduce the number of formal grievances raised	57.7
Other	5.0

Mediation is not appropriate for all issues and ACAS (2008) suggests that it can be used for conflict between employees of the same grade, between Line Managers and their team and between teams or departments. Latreille (2010) takes a more legalistic approach to determining issues that are appropriate and these are shown below.

TABLE 5.2   Perceived suitability for mediation, adapted from Latreille (2010)

Issue	Use (%)
Relationship breakdown	86.8
Bullying or harassment	75.2
Forms of discrimination (other than sex or race)	48.5
Discrimination on the grounds of race	45.0
Discrimination on the grounds of sex	44.8
Conditions of employment	35.9
Discipline	31.1
Pay	27.2
Dismissal	25.6

This cannot be seen as a prescriptive list; some issues, such as bullying and harassment, must be taken on a case-by-case basis and clear cut cases of discrimination or serious bullying and harassment may require more formal processes (ACAS, 2008). In many cases of discipline or dismissal it is not appropriate. Nor is it appropriate in cases where Line Managers are seeking to avoid fulfilling their responsibilities or when employees have disabilities which may prevent them being able to understand the proceeding or express their opinions and feelings clearly.

When establishing a mediation scheme, an employer will have a number of different decisions to make. An employer's decisions may be influenced by:

- the organization's culture;
- the size of the organization;
- the history of conflict;
- previous conflict resolution methods used by that employer; and
- the legal environment.

Whilst supporting the employer in these decisions the HR professional will also need to be mindful of employees' perception of the scheme and procedural justice – this will influence the success of the scheme.

The employer will need to decide on the type of mediation to be used, where to source the mediators, details of the process and the level of formality used. For example, larger organizations may need to have a formal process, clearly publicized to employees, whilst smaller organizations may use mediation more informally.

Types of mediation

There are a number of different approaches to mediation but we will look at the main four:

- In **Facilitative Mediation** the mediator plays an active role in leading parties through a structured process but the parties are responsible for the outcome of the mediation. This is because it is believed that, by making the decisions themselves parties will be more likely to abide by them and the conflict resolved satisfactorily. This is the type of mediation that is most commonly used in the UK.

- In **Directive Mediation** the mediator has greater control over both the process and outcome, making recommendations for the parties; it remains the parties' choice whether to either accept or decline.

- **Evaluative Mediation** is often undertaken by legal advisors: the parties are given some indication of the strengths and weaknesses of the case if it were taken to an Employment Tribunal. This is an approach that attempts to lead parties to a settlement.

- In **Transformative Mediation** (Bush and Folger, 1994) the parties are encouraged to have ownership of the process as well as the final decision. In practice this means that the process is less structured and develops differently for different situations and parties. This approach takes the view that the mediation process may change the way parties behave in the workplace outside of the specific conflict that is being discussed (ACAS, 2008). It sees conflict between parties as a difference in interaction rather than a conflict of interest.

Resources

A mediation scheme can enable issues to be dealt with as they emerge and begin to escalate, well before they fester and positions become established and fixed. This potentially means that problems do not turn into major grievance or discipline issues or lead to tribunal cases. Savings can be made on legal costs for tribunal cases and any award to be made to the claimant if the case were lost. Despite changes in legislation, employment tribunal awards remain costly – the average award for unfair dismissal cases in 2011–12 was £9133 (Ministry of Justice, 2012). The table below shows the average award for discrimination cases in 2011–12.

TABLE 5.3   Awards for discrimination cases 2011–12 (Ministry of Justice, 2012)

Jurisdiction	Award (£)
Race	102,259
Disability	22,183
Age	19,327
Religion	16,725
Sexual Orientation	14, 623
Sex	9,940

However, developing a mediation scheme can still be expensive. A five-day internal mediator course can cost between £1,000 and £2,000 per employee and external mediators can charge around £80 per hour. An estimate of the number of cases requiring mediation will enable an employer to establish a rough guide to costs. Furthermore, internal mediators need ongoing support and cover for outstanding work whilst undertaking their mediation duties. There will also be an increase of administration – arranging appointments and ensuring mediation agreements and other records are stored.

If employees work on a number of small sites or travel around a region then there may be a need to establish key sites with mediators. Employees will have to travel to these mediation sites to attend meetings. The cost and time for employees to travel to the sites needs to be accounted for, and if the employer chooses to have key mediation sites then it is wise to assess whether this affects the uptake of the scheme. An alternative to this is having mediators at all sites, but that will depend on the size and number of sites involved and the available budget.

Establishing a policy and procedure

It is important at this point to determine the factors that may result in the failure of a scheme or reduce the use of the scheme. Some of these are listed as follows:

TABLE 5.4   Factors inhibiting a greater use of mediation, adapted from Latreille (2010)

Factors Inhibiting Greater Use of Mediation	%
Lack of understanding of mediation	21.2
Lack of interest by senior management	12.4
Difficulties finding a mediator	11.8
Cost of Mediation	20.9
Resistance from Line Managers	11.1
Risk of undermining Managers' authority to use disciplinary sanctions	8.8
Lack of support from workforce/Trade Union	4.6
Lack of trust by employees in the mediation process	14.7
Other	6.2

Employees, Line Managers and Senior Managers all need a clear under-standing of a formal scheme. Expectations can include:

- a belief that mediation guarantees a successful resolution and is a panacea for all ills;
- a view that mediation is a weak HR time-wasting exercise before processes are dealt with more formally;
- a mechanism to apportion blame.

It is therefore important to clarify the process of mediation and what it may be able to achieve. We also need to manage expectations of the number of cases, with a realistic estimate of the time employees involved with the process will need to spend away from work. Senior management support is critical to any scheme, but it is necessary to embed the scheme into the normal processes of work, particularly when resources are limited and the process will probably impact on the employee workload. Senior Managers, Line Managers and HR professionals need to ensure that they do not judge the success of the scheme on the results of the most recent mediation, whether that particular mediation has been successful or not in resolving the dispute. A more reasoned approach to determining success of the Mediation Scheme needs to be taken.

When it comes to finding mediators any difficulty could initially be seen as a budgetary issue, as managers do not want to release employees from their work. For the scheme to be a success sufficient internal mediators must be selected and trained. However the post of mediator will be voluntary and particular skills will be needed and that reduces the pool of available em-ployees for the role and so it is not just a budgetary issue. If finding internal mediators is problematic there may be similar difficulty with the availability of external mediators, which is influenced as much by geography as any-thing – rural sites may have greater difficulty finding external mediators than those centrally based in major cities or on good transport networks.

It may be possible that Line Managers may initially resist mediation even if it resolves issues, but in fact there are many logical reasons for resistance. Line Managers will need to release employees for mediation, preventing valuable tasks from being completed and it may be argued affecting the immediate customer. If the issue involves the Line Manager, they may feel that their authority might be undermined and in that case it is important to deal with this sensitively – at times the Line Manager may be correct, and the HR professional needs to support the Line Manager. But at other times the HR professional will know that there is a need for issues to be aired, and the Line Manager needs to feel supported by HR rather than undermined.

Mediation, whilst giving an opportunity to resolve issues does mean that issues are not investigated and grievance or discipline procedures are not followed. If issues are not resolved by mediation then there is still the opportunity to go down the grievance or discipline route, but employees may feel that mediation has unduly delayed this process. In issues of discrimination it may be that the employee, their colleagues or the Trade Union, want to apportion blame rather than resolving issues so that parties can work together. Past experience of management attitudes may influence the view of employees and Trade Unions, and in this case more work needs to be carried out to build trust. If a mediation scheme is to be developed the Trade Union is a key stakeholder and they may be concerned that mediation will make their own role vulnerable.

Formality

Some thought also needs to be given to how employees or Line Managers, if they have a problem, can access mediation. It is suggested that there is a questionnaire available which supplies information about the problem to either HR or a mediation co-ordinator. The information should include the issue that needs mediation and the contact details of the parties. Often with SMEs there is an informal approach to mediation, with the HR professional acting as mediator in some grievances, or when some teams are having intra-group conflict. This can be effective until the HR professional becomes too busy and it may be at this time a more formal scheme is needed.

Internal or external mediators

Employers have the choice either to train employees to become internal mediators or to procure the services of external mediators as and when required, or to do a mixture of both. The Conflict Management Survey (CIPD, 2011) measured the percentage of employers choosing different types of mediators and this is shown below.

FIGURE 5.1   Type of mediator used (CIPD, 2011: 12)

Internal Mediators	42.4%
External Mediators	18.6%
Both	39.0%
Type of Mediator Used (n = 118)	

Decisions are often based on cost – the initial cost of setting up an internal mediation scheme and the long-term fees of external mediation. However there are other factors that should influence that decision. Some of these are identified below:

TABLE 5.5   Internal and external mediators

Internal Mediators	External Mediators
• Easy to supply from employer	• May be more difficult to supply quickly
• Require training and opportunity for experience	• Should have appropriate training and experience to mediate
• Have good understanding of the organizational culture	• Will not have knowledge of the business
• Should be effective as soon as trained and experienced	• Should be effective quickly due to experience
• May not be viewed as impartial	• May have a broader view of the situation
• Knowledge of parties or mediator may affect interaction	• May operate under a national or regional code of conduct
• Parties may find it harder to be open	• Parties may find it easier to be open

The main disadvantage of using an internal mediator is that prior knowledge of parties (or the internal mediator) may affect the way they all interact. Employees may know the internal mediator as a Manager, and have a prior view of their competence. The internal mediator may know the employee and make a judgement on their ability to cooperate. Parties that know the internal mediator may be less open in the process as they may feel that there may be a compromise in confidentiality. For example, if an employee had behaved inappropriately or foolishly they may deny this to an internal mediator when they might have been more open with an external mediator. The main benefit of internal mediators is their familiarity with the context and culture in which the issue occurs and this might enable them to determine the issue quickly.

When seeking external mediators employers may select external consultants, ACAS or solicitors. In the UK mediation remains unregulated. The Civil Mediation Council is the main channel for employment mediation services (CMS, 2009) and registers external providers. There is a Register of Mediators (UKRM), a not-for-profit organization which registers freelance or independent mediators. Mediators registered with UKRM:

- adhere to a Code of Conduct and are subject to a complaints procedure;
- have had 40 hours of nationally accredited training;
- have been assessed on the quality of their work;
- have case supervision to ensure mediators practise within the level of their competence;
- carry out CPD.

(UKRM, 2012)

Nationally accredited training is more difficult to find: for example, there are Level 1 and 2 courses in mediation accredited by the awarding body AIM Awards and ACAS supplies the Certificate in Internal Workplace Mediation which is accredited by the OCR awarding body. However there is a wider range of mediation training providers which are not accredited but may also be suitable for the training of internal mediators.

Guidance

ACAS (2008) recommends guidance is given to both employees and Line Managers and for both, guidance could take the form of a booklet, especially for Line Managers who need to clearly understand the process. For Line Managers ACAS (2008) suggests the following is included:

- What is mediation?
- Why choose mediation?
- When is mediation appropriate?
- Line manager responsibilities and commitment.

There is more to support the employee to decide whether mediation is the right approach for the situation they find themselves in and there is a practical section that helps build a clear idea for them on what to expect. It is important that the employee is aware that the process is voluntary, confidential and 'without prejudice' (this means it will not be referred to in court). The employee needs to know that the final agreement, if made, will be mutually acceptable and is only compulsory at the point it is accepted. Employees should not feel that this is an easy option as it can be very challenging for the parties involved. ACAS (2008) suggests the following could be included:

- What is mediation?
- When is mediation useful?
- How do I decide if mediation is appropriate for me?
- What can I expect?
- The mediation agreement.
- What next?
- Frequently asked questions.

Selecting and training mediators

Not all the volunteers that step forward to take the internal mediator role will be suitable. Mediation requires patience and strong communication skills. ACAS (2008) has listed a range of skills qualities and knowledge:

TABLE 5.6 Skills, qualities, knowledge and experience required by mediators, adapted from ACAS (2008)

Skills	Qualities	Knowledge and Experience
Active listening	Empathetic	Theory of conflict resolution
Oral, written and non-verbal communication	Impartial	Experience of conflict resolution
Questioning	Approachable	Understanding of equality and diversity issues
Observing	Non-judgemental	Understanding of HR policies and procedures
Reasoning	Professional	Knowledge of power and minority issues

TABLE 5.6 *continued*

Skills	Qualities	Knowledge and Experience
Summarizing	Honest	Experience of facilitating informal groups
Reflecting	Creative	Knowledge of the mediation process
Problem-solving	Credible	An awareness of the legal context of mediation
Building rapport	Flexible	Some knowledge of employee relations
Facilitating	Integrity	
Reframing		
Objectivity		
Information analysis		
Time management		
Conflict Management		
Negotiation		
Following procedures		
Organizing		
Generating options		

Knowledge and experience can be gained through training and opportunities for internal mediators to mediate. Skills can be developed but the stronger the skill set an internal mediator possesses before starting out, the more effective they will be. It is the qualities of the internal mediator that are most important, and these will be central to your selection of the right internal mediator.

The approach to recruiting and selecting internal mediators will be similar to any other recruitment and selection process. It is necessary to identify the essential and desirable criteria for the role. There may be other criteria as well – the employer may need internal mediators to be based at different sites or want to have internal mediators at different levels so that there is a range of mediators from which to pick when the need arises. It is also necessary to determine whether individuals will apply directly or be nominated by their Line Manager. It may be helpful to prepare a job description, as this enables practical issues to be thought through: for example, it may be necessary to identify if there should be a time limit on the extent each mediator would be used to reflect an understanding of the impact the role would have on their other work.

Once these are determined then the recruitment can go ahead and this may coincide or be immediately subsequent to the launch of the scheme. Interviews will be carried out and internal mediators selected.

Training

We have already discussed the training available for mediators, but to add detail to this we may need to identify some of the important areas that should be included in any training. At a minimum:

- knowledge of conflict resolution;
- knowledge of the mediation process;
- the opportunity to practise mediation skills using, for example, case studies and role-play exercises;
- knowledge of the issues surrounding diversity and the legal context (so that mediators understand the boundaries of mediation).

If external training is to be provided then there will also need to be an induction by the employer to the processes that the organization will be using – how employees will seek mediation, the mediation agreement, record keeping and support. Training is also required for employees and Line Managers so that they are aware of the scheme and what mediation can offer.

Stages of mediation

Mediation can be separated into five stages. Both ACAS (2008) and Gaitan and Kleiner (1999) have provided guidance.

Stage One

At the first stage parties are met separately and the ground rules are established. The aim is for the mediator to listen to their story and to determine what each party wants to achieve through the mediation. This gives the mediator an opportunity to explain what mediation can and cannot achieve and to explain the process to both parties.

Stage Two

Once trust has been established with the mediator, each party meets alone with the mediator. The aim of this stage is for both parties to be able to explain their story without interruption, apart from any questions by the mediator for the purpose of clarifying the story to the other party. The mediator will discuss the problem with both parties alone – they will then identify the key areas of disagreement (and agreement) and will determine what will be discussed later. By determining 'wants' and 'needs', it is possible for both parties to begin to understand the motivation behind the other parties' actions.

Stage Three

After each party has had the opportunity to give their view to the mediator both sides meet together with the mediator who facilitates their understanding and empathy for the other party's position. This is a difficult stage and the mediator may need to intervene to maintain a positive and safe environment, which meets the ground rules agreed to at Stage One, whilst at the same time allowing for open and frank expression of feeling. This requires careful judgement to guide individuals to a better understanding, both of themselves and their own reaction and that of others. This is the most challenging, and usually the longest, stage of the process.

The mediator at this stage needs to actively listen, summarizing or clarifying when necessary. It is at this stage that the mediator may support parties by reframing issues. Reframing is providing another viewpoint on an issue or point (issues that are clear to one party may be viewed from a totally different perspective by another party). The mediator will need to help parties view actions from different perspectives while remaining impartial.

If the meeting is not promoting movement in the positions of each party then it is wise to meet with each party separately again. This maintains trust and confidentiality and enables the mediator to identify any impasse and determine possible solutions to it without the other party being present.

Stage Four

At this stage consensus has nearly been achieved. The parties need to determine the practical issues that require resolving and, using problem solving techniques, the mediator helps the parties identify what needs to be done. Any agreement will be made in writing as a formal mediation agreement.

Stage Five

The meeting is closed, with both parties being given a copy of the agreement. It is important to clarify any change in behaviour or any action that each party has promised to undertake.

Managing the process

Launching the scheme

It is necessary to think about the way in which the scheme is communicated to employees. If the scheme is informal, Line Managers and employees still need to know that it is available. Often schemes are not publicized as in reality resources would not be able to meet demand. This is not a good reason to avoid publicizing an informal scheme – discussions need to be held with senior management for appropriate resources. If there is an official launch of the scheme then it may be easier to recruit internal mediators and it shows that the employer is fully supportive. However, it does mean that the employer and HR professional are more exposed to any failure of the scheme. A small-scale approach to the scheme may make both the HR professional and employer more comfortable, but in fact this may adversely affect the success of the scheme if employees and Line Managers do not know it is available or what is involved. A small-scale start may be wise to gauge uptake and to ensure that the right number of internal mediators is recruited so that they all are able to have enough ongoing experience. There are a number of different factors influencing the decision on how to launch the scheme and therefore the decision is one for the individual employer.

Administration and support

Carrying out mediation is a difficult task and if internal mediators are used then it is necessary for them to have some support to discuss issues and debrief. Many employers recruit a mediation co-ordinator, either full- or part-time. This co-ordinator will ensure requests for mediation are matched with a mediator, that arrangements are made within the specified timescale and that records and agreements are filed, and appointments made.

Managing non-resolution

When issues are not resolved then the situation may need to progress to more formal processes, either grievance or discipline as appropriate. The mediation scheme procedure should provide the opportunity for the HR professional to meet with the employee (in cases that would go on to grievance) or with the Line Manager (for cases that would be appropriate for discipline) to determine whether a formal process is appropriate. If this is not carried out then the employee may claim that the grievance was known about but nothing was done, and may resign and claim constructive dismissal. If a discipline is appropriate but is not followed through then this undermines the Line Manager and communicates to employees that mediation is a way to avoid discipline proceedings.

It is important to be aware of the fact that mediation is a confidential process and notes from mediation cannot be used as evidence either in the internal investigation or for an Employment Tribunal claim. Also mediators should not be called as witnesses in an Employment Tribunal claim. It is acceptable that the Employment Tribunal is aware that the case has been mediated but that should be the extent of their knowledge.

The checklist below supports HR professionals to prepare a mediation procedure:

TABLE 5.7 Checklist for mediation procedure

1. Is the Mediation Policy and Procedure in writing?	Yes/No
2. Have employees been given a guidance booklet?	Yes/No
3. Have Line Managers been given a guidance booklet?	Yes/No
4. Does the procedure and guidance booklet explain how employees are to seek mediation?	Yes/No
5. Does the procedure establish how long they may wait to hear about their mediation meeting?	Yes/No
6. Does the procedure state that employees will be invited in writing to a meeting and how long the process might take?	Yes/No
7. Does the procedure state what training mediators are to be given and how often or if external mediators are being used, where they are to be supplied from?	Yes/No
8. Does the procedure state how internal mediators are selected for a particular mediation and in what circumstances a mediator is not suitable?	Yes/No
9. Does the procedure state how complaints about mediators will be managed?	Yes/No
10. Does the procedure explain the support that is provided for internal mediators?	Yes/No
11. Does the procedure explain what records are maintained?	Yes/No
12. Does the procedure have a sample mediation agreement?	Yes/No
13. Does the procedure explain what may happen if resolution is not achieved?	Yes/No
14. Does the mediation policy and procedure link clearly to the grievance and discipline policy and any other relevant HR procedures?	Yes/No

The scenario below describes a typical issue in which mediation can support communication and understanding between different parties.

Scenario

Tiners Ltd

Tiners Ltd is a construction company established in 1985, focusing on the manufacture and installation of double-glazed windows and conservatories. It has a national customer base which has been hard-won in this competitive business, with sales made in particular through repeat business or recommendation – it is a business where both product quality and customer service are paramount.

During the recession sales of both products have decreased and the company has had to make a small number of redundancies, with the main problem being slow cash flow and limited sales. Whilst there is enough profit to make monthly staff payments, suppliers are also short of funds and so push for shorter credit terms.

The Manufacturing Manager has worked in this role for many years and has learnt the value of manufacturing a high quality product. His steady conscientious approach to his work has been instilled into his team, with whom he has built a good relationship over the years. Anxious to do a good job he ensures his team is thoroughly trained in reading architects' scale drawings and in quality assurance; there are very few recalls of his double-glazing or conservatories.

The Operations Manager is tied to time constraints and his teams are less well trained. His aim is to take as little time as possible to construct on-site as 'time is money'. He admits that his team cuts corners, but not on the areas that the planning inspector may assess, and so he can move his team onto the next job and be seen as being both efficient and effective.

Finally, the Sales and Customer Services Manager, a confident and socially able man, is keen to be spontaneous and to promise anything for a good sale, which the Architect and the Manufacturing Manager then need to

▶

adapt to make it feasible. He naturally focuses his attention on sales, particularly in this economic climate, so that he is seen as vital to the company's future. Customer Service is in his view the Cinderella service as it does not bring in any further money. Lately there has been an increase in the number of complaints and difficulties that he has to manage.

The three managers have disagreed more recently and the CEO is concerned that the different approaches to work may cause a more long-term problem and that their disagreements are beginning to adversely affect the teams. For example, the manufacturing team dislikes the approach taken by those working on-site and feels that complaints that have been initially sent to manufacturing are really the fault of the Operations Manager and his teams. The CEO has suggested mediation and arranged for external mediators to visit for one day.

The mediator met with all three parties separately to determine the issues and then they met all together. They were able to see that they had different personalities and different priorities but that they all contributed to the future viability of the company. They also recognized that the economic situation had put extra pressure on their working relationships, a pressure that made any differences in approach seem more acute. Though the Manufacturing Manager still wanted to take time to ensure good quality, he came to acknowledge the importance, for the viability of the company, of a steady flow of work. This made him more amenable to these difficult projects. The Operations Manager agreed to make sure his team did not cut corners if the CEO would agree an extra half-day on site for conservatories. More importantly, the OM realized the effect that cutting corners was having on both repeat customer and recommendation sales. The most valuable part of the agreement was the decision to meet regularly to discuss issues and the mediator made sure that the date, venue and time of the first meeting was set before concluding.

Additional resources

ACAS provides a short video on mediation which may be beneficial for both Line Managers and employees to view. It can be accessed at **http://www.acas.org.uk/index.aspx?articleid=2825.**

Conflict – collective dispute resolution

HR professionals working in a non-unionized setting cannot ignore collective dispute resolution skills. Having the knowledge and skills to work with Unions improves our employability, and our career paths may well lead us into situations where we need to understand how collective bargaining is carried out.

Collective bargaining

Collective bargaining is collective negotiation by the Union on behalf of its members. It is a formal process for the two parties, the employee representative and the employer, to present and discuss the proposal to changes in terms and conditions of employment with the purpose of finding agreement.

Preparing for collective bargaining

The first step for any negotiation commences a long time before any formal negotiation starts. It is imperative to build a good working relationship with Union representatives at all times. Listening to them if they have an issue that needs your assistance, and treating them with respect will have established a foundation which will help the negotiation process. This will ensure that both sides approach the negotiation in a more positive manner.

Prior to the negotiation the employer may find it difficult to determine what the claims of the Union may be. It could be that a pay agreement is coming to an end in which case it is probable that any negotiations will have an element of pay claim. Though the employer may have had less time to prepare for the negotiation, the Union will have requested information from the employer which may well have provided a clue to the argument the Union may be wishing to make. The employer will need to have a good idea of the current practices and procedures and existing agreements. This gives a basis on which negotiations can be made.

The approach that the Trade Union will make will depend on the original agreement between employer and Union. It may be that a letter informs the employer of the claim, or that the Trade Union requests a meeting with Management in which it makes a claim. In either circumstance it provides the employer with the information the employer needs to prepare more thoroughly for the negotiation. Only then can the employer establish their own aims for the negotiation and anticipate what the aims of the Union might be.

One tool that may be useful is the aspiration grid (Gennard and Judge, 2010). This tool can be used to identify the position of both parties. In the example below the employer has surmised that the Union will argue strongly for a wage increase, but if necessary the employer would be prepared to agree. This is an integrative bargaining issue – there is the possibility of common ground. There is a likelihood of finding common ground with the holiday increase also. However, there is one issue where there is no scope for any change in position. The employer wishes to instigate performance-related pay whatever happens. If the employer has interpreted the Union's position correctly then it clearly shows that there are two very important issues – the wage increase for the Union and Performance-Related Pay for the employer. Other issues are less important to either party. By identifying the issues in which there is little scope for agreement the employer can try to analyze why these areas are particularly important to each party. In doing this the employer might find that there may, in fact, be some room for manoeuvre on these issues or that there is a different way to manage the same issue so that both parties are content. It enables the employer to be flexible before positions have been set and any change being seen as defeat.

TABLE 5.8 The aspiration grid adapted from Gennard and Judge (2010: 395)

Items for negotiations	Union			Employer		
	Ideal	Real	Fall-back	Fall-back	Real	Ideal
Wage increase 2%	X	X	X	0	X	X
Holiday increased by 2 days	X	X	0	0	0	X
Performance Related Pay	0	0	X	X	X	X
Pension payments increased by 1%	X	0	0	0	X	X

Roles

The negotiation requires more than just the Lead Negotiator. A member of the team will record what has been agreed and take notes during the meetings with the Union. The Record Keeper will also take notes at the employer's meetings so that any decisions on strategy or objectives are clear and can be laid out for the Lead Negotiator prior to the meetings with the Union. The Observer takes a dispassionate viewpoint, will quietly examine the negotiation and so will be able to give feedback and advice to the Lead Negotiator. The Specialist has technical expertise which can be used to advise the Lead Negotiator on, for example, financial or legal matters. The Specialist may also seek an adjournment if they need to advise the Lead Negotiator further. There may be an Analyst who will review Union offers and analyze the effect of these on the business. Finally, one of the negotiation team will need to be responsible for the environmental issues, for example ensuring the heating and ventilation in the room is adequate or reminding the Lead Negotiator that the discussion has been lengthy and the parties may appreciate a break. So the team could consist of:

- a Lead Negotiator;
- a Record Keeper;
- an Observer;
- a Specialist;
- an Analyst.

Negotiation skills

Carrying out a negotiation is a particularly difficult task, requiring a range of high-level skills. It needs the negotiator to manage complex and detailed information, both as part of the preparation and during the negotiation. Information at the preparation stage will need to be analyzed so that a strong counter-argument can be developed. Information during the negotiation is provided by the Union as part of their argument, and this may need an immediate reply or, if necessary, require scrutiny before a response is given.

Of course, any response given will require perception and good judgement. A negotiator will require the ability to evaluate information and assess its value to the employer's position and to effectively gauge what can be offered to the Union and what is of too great a value to give away. A good negotiator will carry out the negotiations by building on their excellent interpersonal skills. They will be astute and emotionally intuitive, with an awareness of other people's feelings, which they can use as they carry out the exchange. They will also possess patience and integrity, to be able to build rapport and empathy and to be able to effectively illustrate verbally.

Flexibility and creativity are essential so that the problem can be viewed from the different positions of the parties. They then can identify whether the needs of both parties have aspects that can be accommodated, whether their needs have aspects that could be viewed as complimentary in any way, and suggest solutions to facilitate a win-win situation. They will possess commercial awareness – an understanding of the needs of the business, so that they can interpret the information gathered in the exchange to make suggestions that fulfil their aims.

The collective bargaining meetings

Once the Union claim has been received, either in the form of a letter or during a first meeting, the employer has a reasonable idea of the key issues. The employer will prepare its response, forming an idea of the possible reaction the Union may have to the position of the employer, before arranging another meeting with the Union.

A series of meetings with the Union follow in which different parties discuss the issues broadly, using clarifying questions as required. It is important to use these meetings effectively to get a good understanding of the issues and the importance of them to the Union, and it may be that the employer may later return to the aspiration grid to make amendments that influence the offers that are made. Summarizing using neutral language helps both parties ensure they have a full understanding but does not judge in any way the arguments made.

Gradually during these meetings the views of both sides become clear and the parties begin to link issues that could be traded and make suggestions. Signalling a trade is not always easy and often negotiators will use the phrase 'if...then' as this identifies the linked issues. This stage should not be rushed – the Record Keeper will take notes and in an adjournment the Analyst will provide an assessment of the consequences of accepting the offer to the employer. The Lead Negotiator should give way on those issues that are less costly to the employer but of value to the Union. For example, it may be less costly to give all employees in the bargaining unit a one per cent pay rise than to give them all one day's extra holiday. If signals are identified either party may move their position to make a tentative agreement.

Adjournments are important as they give each party an opportunity to assess the situation and inform others of their progress as necessary. Adjournments may be as short as half an hour or as long as a few days, but the purpose of the adjournment is to:

- enable the team to evaluate proposals;
- regroup the team and reassess strategy;
- confer with those in higher authority.

It needs to be remembered that the Union Negotiator will need to return to the Union members to get the agreement ratified.

The position of both parties progressively comes nearer until an agreement can be made. Just before this both parties should make sure that they clarify the issues and the agreement fully. The employer should convince the Union that this offer is final.

The case study below describes some of the issues between the Rail Maritime and Transport Union (RMT) and Transport for London (TfL) in the summer of 2012 in which the Olympics were held.

CASE STUDY   Rail Maritime and Transport Union and the Olympics

The summer of 2012 saw London hosting the Olympics, so an effective transport system was vital. However it was also clear that with the numbers of visitors using TfL there was a great deal of profit to be made. The Rail, Maritime and Transport (RMT) Union not only wanted a share of these profits for their members but also used the opportunity to bring up inequities that could be resolved at this time. Therefore, the RMT Union had strong leverage in a negotiation as any failure to resolve the dispute would result in a strike over the Olympic period, with the disruption and bad press that would entail, along with a loss of profit for TfL.

The negotiations continued throughout Spring 2012. Initially the Tube drivers were offered a bonus of £400 for working the Olympic period, with some of the payment linked to the achievement of certain targets, but this was declined by the RMT Union. Finally they accepted an offer of a bonus for Tube drivers of up to £1,000, with no change to existing agreements or terms and conditions. However, the dispute continued over the implementation of the payment and the use of casual staff during the Olympics.

On 11 June, 19 July and 27 July there were ballots in which the relevant bargaining unit members supported strike action. The RMT balloted cleaners for equal Olympic bonuses in line with other staff, a sick-pay scheme, free travel passes and improvements to the pension scheme, with the threat of industrial action. The cleaners on the Tube and Docklands Light Railway took strike action and picketed throughout the Olympics and in December 2012 there was still no resolution to the dispute. (Adapted from reports made by the RMT Union, 2013)

Industrial action

In the event of receiving notification of strike action you will need to advise the Line Managers who have members of their team who are taking industrial action. Line Managers will need to discuss the action with their team so that they are aware of the details of when the action will take place, that the action is legal and that those that are not part of the Union may need to cross a picket line to attend work. Non-Union members will need to know that any unauthorized absence will be treated under the discipline procedure. They will also be required to maintain good relations with both Union and Non-Union members as the team will need to work together after the strike is over.

The first step will be to discover whether there has been a prior agreement with the Union over the procedure during a strike. There may be a protocol agreed, which covers some of the more challenging or complex issues that industrial action might create. There could be an agreement made for how the HR department will manage any sickness absence or annual leave during a strike – for example, it would be sensible to make it clear whether a striking employee should continue to follow sickness absence procedures during the industrial action and be subject to a return to work interview once the action has ceased. The agreement might cover other aspects of industrial action, such as the wording of internal and external communication concerning the action. Depending on the size of the company, and its significance in the local community, there might be press coverage. Whilst the protocol could give details of external communication, it may also give guidance on how to manage employees that make comments to the press about the strike and the employer.

The next step is to check that the action is legal, and this may involve taking legal advice to confirm that the ballot has been carried out correctly. The type of action, whether a strike or action short of a strike, should be confirmed, along with the dates, duration and employees involved. This establishes the scope of the action so that contingency planning can be carried out.

Whilst it is clear that recruitment agencies cannot legally recruit temporary staff to cover for striking employees, there are other options that may be available to the employer. There is no legal constraint on the employer if it wishes to recruit temporary staff directly, rather than through an agency, though from a practical point of view in the short period before industrial action this may be difficult. It is possible for an employer to redeploy employees from one team to cover another. However, employees cannot be forced to complete tasks that are outside their job description and they might not have the training to carry out the work. Even willing employees that are redeployed to cover may not find it easy crossing a picket line in this situation and it is important to remember that the employer has a duty of care to its employees and putting them in this situation may be a matter of judgement.

Line Managers will be required to make contingency plans in which different departments will play their part. For example the industrial action may impact on delays in orders or delivery times and customers may need to be notified. The website may need to provide information about this and customer services may provide assistance passing information to customers. Any suppliers making deliveries should be warned that there is a picket line and encouraged to allow extra time for their journey. Some suppliers may not wish to cross the picket line but by making contact with them the company may be able to encourage them to do so, in order to reduce the negative impact of the strike.

Conclusion

We have focused on the planning and skills required for managing disputes, both individual and collective. HR professionals have to manage grievances between the employer and employee and both Line Managers and HR professionals are often called on to mediate between employees. Formal mediation schemes are becoming a useful means of handling some of these situations. When managing collective disputes the HR profession will need to develop their negotiation skills to ensure that both parties leave with satisfactory results so that relations between the employer and the Trade Union can remain positive. Whilst some Trade Unions remain militant, using the threat of industrial action as leverage, others build a partnership with employers, being a representative voice for their members but taking a more active role in the organization. Other employers choose to develop non-Union voice mechanisms, such as the Employee Forum. The situation of each employer is unique and the choices made in terms of managing the employment relationship will differ, but every employer will benefit from a planned and skilled approach to Employee Relations.

The next chapter examines how the employment relationship can be measured to provide information for employers from which they can determine any problems. But before that the case study below analyzes the Employee Forum at Prudential and how it was used practically to support both Prudential and give employees a voice.

CASE STUDY   Employee Forum at Prudential

The Employee Forum at Prudential, established as a response to legislation, has been a key mechanism for collective voice. Initially it was involved in a change programme entailing difficult decisions about restructuring. Being needed in such a practical activity provided an opportunity for the Forum to show that its contributions are valuable, and it also allowed the Prudential to meet its requirements for consultation.

Following its contribution as a consultation tool, it was clear that there was an opportunity to use the Employee Forum in a proactive role in engagement. There has been a cultural shift in Prudential whereby employees have become more involved in decision-making; the Employee Forum has had a role in this. One area it has worked on is the internal Prudential brand, helping to identify what employees value and this has led to 'Prudential's People Principles' which details the culture and core values of the company.

The support of the Executive Team has been paramount to the success of the Employee Forum. Management find it helpful as a gauge of employees' views and Employee Forum Representatives find that not only does it give the opportunity for employees to make a difference but also to feel valued for their opinions and input.

Representatives have adapted to meet the needs of the company – there are now Lead and Specialist Representatives who have direct relationships with key stakeholders and have an understanding of a particular function or operation. Pulse Representatives have their attention on the pulse of the organization and report back on a monthly basis. Communication to employees is through the quarterly Employee Newsletter and the Employee Zone hub, with its Employee Forum e-mail box.

This approach to an Employee Forum is very different from the traditional approach in which the Forum would become an opportunity for grumbles and complaints, rather than an effective tool for dealing with issues. This is not to say that Prudential's Employee Forum did not raise grumbles at the start but it is now much more positive. The difference is the genuine commitment from top management, the scope of decision-making given, the effective structure of the Employee Forum and the communication of value to employees.

(Adapted from research carried out by IPA and Tomorrow's Company, 2012)

DIAGNOSTIC QUESTIONNAIRE   Negotiation

This questionnaire is designed to support HR professionals to evaluate your own negotiation skills.

		Yes	No
1	I am able to analyze written and verbal information to identify the key issues.	☐	☐
2	I calmly manage complex written and verbal reports and data.	☐	☐
3	I can identify the employer's response to a range of different arguments.	☐	☐
4	I communicate clearly and concisely.	☐	☐
5	I ask questions to ensure I have a clear understanding.	☐	☐
6	I can see issues from a range of viewpoints.	☐	☐
7	I enjoy identifying common ground.	☐	☐
8	I think clearly under pressure.	☐	☐
9	I create a professional and comfortable environment.	☐	☐
10	In a negotiation I do not take comments personally.	☐	☐
11	In a negotiation I treat all parties with respect.	☐	☐
12	I am able to identify when there is signalling.	☐	☐
13	I am willing to compromise when needed.	☐	☐
14	I can identify important objectives and can adapt strategies to achieve them.	☐	☐
15	I can see when it is time to stop negotiating and make an agreement.	☐	☐

Scores

Questions 1–4 relate principally to negotiation preparation, questions 5–11 relate to the exchange with the Union and questions 11–15 relate to the last stages of the negotiation.

Between 15 and 13 positive answers

To achieve this score you are an experienced negotiator, whether at work or outside, or have developed the key skills to enable you to negotiate well. You prepare effectively, managing complex information to see clearly the strategy that you need to take. If you have answered these questions positively then it is likely you are a confident communicator, assertive but not aggressive. You also are reasonably able to end the negotiation effectively, making timely decisions. However this questionnaire has not assessed your ability to work with other people during the negotiation and it may be that this is an area you can develop further.

Between 12 and 9 positive answers
To get a score of 12 it is likely that you are a reasonably confident communicator having gained the majority of your marks from questions 5–11. The distribution of your scores between preparation and the end of the negotiation process will provide information for you to assess your ability. Often negotiators are good at planning, analyzing the information and forming the strategy that should be taken, but find it difficult to identify when to compromise and make the final decision to agree. They may either finish too early, not getting the best bargain, or leave it too long and begin to irritate the other party. Alternatively you are able to continue negotiations as necessary, and have good social skills, but you are weaker at the more theoretical analysis, planning and information management in the preparation stage. A lower score again depends on the distribution but at 9 positive answers you probably remain reasonably good at communication, but are weaker at both preparation and the end of the negotiation.

Between 8 and 2 positive answers
A score of 8 positive answers could theoretically show someone good both at preparation and decision-making but this is very unlikely. Most negotiators have a degree of communication skills but these may need developing further. They may also have some decision-making skills, but may not always identify when the other party is signalling to them or end the negotiation at the best time. These skills take time and experience to develop.

A score of between 3–7 shows a new negotiator with some good points but it is unlikely you are yet able to clearly identify signalling or end the negotiation at the right time. However each negotiation provides opportunity to develop your skills and the questionnaire will have high-lighted areas you can now concentrate on.

If you scored below 3 it is likely that you have assessed your-self very harshly – these questions need a general answer. You do not need to be perfect but answer positively where in the majority of cases you meet the question. It may be worth reassessing your answers.

Measurement

06

INTRODUCTION

Human Relations is a dynamic profession and it is only relatively recently that Employee Relations specialists have progressed from being reactive to developing more strategic approaches. This has moved apace with the propensity of research on employee engagement, and corporate measurement of the employment relationship has tended to focus on engagement as a measure that can be linked to productivity. There are also national surveys that support both companies and national policy makers.

This chapter does not delve into the measurement of engagement but will explore:

- the challenges faced by companies preparing to assess the employment relationship;
- national surveys and their value to employers;
- specific findings from the Workplace Employment Relations Study (Van Wanrooy *et al*, 2013);
- qualitative and quantitative measures available to employers.

The challenge of measurement

The rationale for measurement

Employers will want to measure the health of the employment relationship in order to make sure that they attract potential employees of the right calibre and retain them within the organization. Despite the current global recession, in which it could be assumed that recruitment and retention activities are easier for employers, acquiring and retaining skilled staff continues to be hard for UK business, affecting the employers' competitiveness in an already demanding market. Monitoring and taking steps to improve the state of the employment relationship has a direct influence on the competitiveness of the business.

It may also be important to an organization that they are seen to monitor the employment relationship and to be seen to act on the information that is gathered. It gives a message to employees that their views matter. Currently, most assessment of the employment relationship is by means of the measurement of engagement, using employee attitude surveys. If these surveys are based on Gallup Q12 the results can be compared with over 400 other companies. There are also standardized questionnaires but these tend to focus on specific areas such as engagement or job satisfaction. Also consultancies provide specific diagnostic services to measure engagement or employee relations. For example the Employee Quality of Working Life Survey (Albrecht, 2013) is a standardized test for organizations providing measures on stress, work-related quality of life and engagement.

A number of national surveys are also available. These can provide information for employers to, if not benchmark against, at least have a view of the state of Employee Relations, the psychological contract and the employment relationship in other companies and sectors.

Validity and reliability

Most employers design their own employee attitude survey. One of the challenges with any organizational survey is its validity – that the questions test what they set out to test. There is a danger that employees will choose answers that they believe the employer wants them to give. The ability for employees to answer the questions anonymously supports the validity; however, the extent to which employees in all organizations feel secure enough to answer truthfully, despite promised anonymity, remains questionable. In fact it could be argued that it is in companies where the employment relationship is best that the response in attitude surveys may be the most candid.

The challenge of reliability – the ability to get the same answer if the questionnaire is repeated, is less controversial. If we can depend on the results to indicate the attitude of the workforce at that point in time, then if it was repeated during that time period the results should be the same. It can be argued that validity and reliability are best managed with surveys that are externally designed and administered as this can enhance the questionnaire's credibility.

Designing an in-house survey

Before we go on to look at questionnaire design it is important to understand that this is not our only option for gaining information about employee satisfaction. We have data available from exit interviews which can provide valuable information for why employees have left, and if we are to carry out some primary research of our own, we also could use interviews with employees, along with focus groups, to gather the views of employees. The benefit of a questionnaire is its anonymity – our role as HR professional makes it difficult for employees to be truly objective in their answers in an interview or focus group, regardless of how much we encourage honest answers. Employees that are interviewed or part of a focus group may feel that any complaint about the company might be passed on to their managers, or that if they are viewed as someone who is not fully satisfied with the company, it might compromise their position if there was an opportunity for a promotion. For these reasons a questionnaire is often chosen.

For many organizations an in-house survey is sufficient and this can be designed with some thought. A survey needs to be clearly constructed, with questions which are not ambiguous. When preparing an in-house survey we are able to focus our questions so that particular issues pertinent to the company can be explored in greater depth. We also need to be concerned that any questions that we as the organization may ask will not engender expectations that then cannot be met.

When preparing employee engagement and satisfaction surveys it is necessary that we keep in mind the need for:

- clarity;
- comparability long-term;
- relevance.

Make sure that questions are clear; this may be particularly important for MNCs, which may have problems with translation and cultural differences in answering particularly culturally specific questions. Findings will need to be comparable over time to show the impact of interventions made to improve employee satisfaction and engagement. Finally questions need to be relevant to the organization and the focus it will take – often less problematic for those surveys developed in-house.

Survey design principles

There are some general points which can make questionnaires easier to complete and help improve the response rate:

- make sure that they have a logical sequence;
- separate questions into sections;
- make the questionnaire short;
- number the pages;
- make the questionnaire attractive.

Questions can be closed, or fixed responses in which the respondent chooses between a selection of fixed answers. These are usually easy to answer and so are best placed at the beginning of the section of questions. They provide quantifiable information, which is easy to present but does not give the depth of information that is needed to make improvements. Examples of closed questions are given below:

Have you ever had a formal grievance?
Yes ☐   No ☐

What is your opinion of training provision?
Excellent   Poor
1   2   3   4   5

Open questions give employees the opportunity to give their own perspective and can enable the HR Professional to gather information that was not anticipated. This is particularly valuable.

Using surveys

When it is time to release an employee survey it can be publicized using the company intranet. It may be that it is given to all employees or a selection – if a sample is chosen then these will usually be randomly selected, or if there are issues in one part of the organization then it may be that only employees from this area are chosen. Questionnaires can be set up on the intranet so that employees can open and answer them anonymously, or they can be sent by email. This email acts as a covering letter and so must explain:

- the purpose of the study;
- anonymity – especially if they have been contacted by email;
- the timescale for response;
- a 'thank you'!

Once the information has been gathered it is Management which will need to decide how they should respond to the views aired in the survey. Doing nothing is not an option – if the employer does not respond then the employees will know that it was not a true consultation and it will damage the trust built between the organization and the employees. This is a particular problem of surveys that are led by one department, such as the HR department, with little commitment from the Senior Management Team.

National measures of the employment relationship

There are a number of different providers of surveys and information that can be used to analyze, compare and discuss the state of Employee Relations, the psychological contract and the employment relationship. CIPD research by Guest and Conway (2002) provided some benchmarks for companies over a period of six years but this is now a little dated. The CIPD produces a quarterly Employee Outlook which provides a snapshot of the employment relationship on a national scale. Also the Chartered Management Institute publishes an annual research report, 'The Quality of Working Life in the UK'.

However the best respected is the Workplace Employment Relations Study, of which the most recent is the 2011 survey.

How WERS 2011 was carried out

The Workplace Employment Relations Study (Van Wanrooy *et al*, 2013), conducted in 2011, provides an indication of the Employment Relationship on a national scale and offers the opportunity to compare changes in employee relationships since 1980. The study interviewed 2,680 Managers, 1,002 worker representatives and 21,981 employees. The researchers believe that the sample taken is representative of all British workplaces of five or more employees, and of 90 per cent of employees. It is carried out every four years, with preliminary findings produced before a more detailed final report is published. It is used to inform Government policy and future research.

The main preliminary findings of the WERS 2011 study

The findings are quite extensive for our purposes and so we will look at three main areas:

- response to Recession;
- discontent in the Workplace;
- employment Representation.

Response to recession

In the first findings of the WERS study (Van Wanrooy *et al*, 2013), the researchers looked at the effect the recession had on UK businesses. The sectors most affected by the recession have been Construction, Transport, Communication, Financial Services and Public Administration, although very few sectors have survived unscathed.

In this recession larger companies have found it necessary to take some action to overcome the effects of the recession, with some smaller companies taking no action. This has meant that a large percentage of employees (89 per cent) have experienced some effects from the recession. Whilst some businesses closed, the percentage was no different than in the previous study. The financial impact has been felt more by employees, with organizations working hard to resist the need for compulsory redundancies and the loss of skills that this entails. According to employees, their wages were cut or frozen (33 per cent) and their workload increased (29 per cent). In such an environment it could be expected that discontent would be increased but as the following section shows this was not the case.

Discontent in the workforce

Despite the challenging economic situation, and the need for organizations to restructure and make redundancies in the period of the study there was no reflection of this in the satisfaction of employees. In fact relations between management and employees improved very slightly.

TABLE 6.1 How businesses responded to recession in 2008
(WERS, 2013)

	Private (%)	Public (%)	All (%)
Freeze or cut in wages	39	63	42
Freeze filling vacant posts	26	44	28
Change in the organization of work	22	35	24
Postpone workforce expansion	21	22	21
Reduce paid overtime	17	23	18
Reduce training expenditure	14	32	16
Reduce use of agency staff	13	31	16
Reduce basic hours	16	6	15
Compulsory redundancies	14	9	14
Voluntary redundancies	5	23	7
Reduce non-wage benefits	7	7	7
Enforced unpaid leave	3	2	3
Increase use of agency staff	2	4	3
Other response	3	5	3
No action taken	26	11	24

TABLE 6.2 Relationship between managers and employees
(WERS, 2013)

	2004	2011
Managers rating relations as good or very good	93%	96%
Employees rating relations as good or very good	62%	64%

The incidence of employees taking strike action increased from one per cent to four per cent, an equivalent increase from 905,000 working days lost to 1.39 million working days lost. This is attributable mainly to public sector strike action in response to the Government's austerity measures.

TABLE 6.3   Measures of discontent (WERS, 2013)

	2004	2011
Percentage of workplaces using disciplinary action	43%	39%
Percentage of workplaces receiving employee grievances	38%	30%
Percentage of working days lost to absence	3.5%	3.7%
Percentage of workplaces making dismissals	19%	17%
Percentage of employees leaving workplaces voluntarily	15%	10%

At first sight these results seem to be promising reductions that may show an improvement in the employment relationship. However the results may merely reflect the need for employees to retain their jobs, unable to voice grievances and working hard to prevent disciplinary action in order to prevent being perceived as troublesome employees. In fact the reduction in the percentage of employees leaving voluntarily from an organization clearly indicates that organizations are maintaining a stable workforce, which has benefits for organizations in terms of recruitment costs and training, but also shows the difficulty that employees have in finding new jobs.

Employee representation

Four types of employee representation were assessed in the WERS survey (Van Wanrooy *et al*, 2013): Union membership, Joint Consultative Committees, European Works Councils and other Non-Union employee representation.

As Table 6.4 shows, there has been a small decline in Union membership. Though the change in percentage of employees belonging to a Union is insignificant, there is a more noticeable drop in Unions recognized in the different workplaces except for the public sector where there Union presence is constant. This implies that where there are Unions, often in larger establishments, membership is strong. The drop in Union recognition in the private sector has been in smaller organizations.

TABLE 6.4 Measures of Union presence (WERS, 2013)

	2004	2011
Percentage of employees belonging to a Trade Union	32%	30%
Workplace with any Union presence – private manufacturing	23%	14%
Workplace with any Union presence – private services	20%	14%
Workplace with any Union presence – public sector	90%	90%

The percentage of workplaces using Joint Consultative Committees continued to drop in all instances including the public sector as Table 6.5 shows. There is also a decline, though very small, in the use of European Works Councils in those organizations with an international presence.

TABLE 6.5 Measures of other collective representation (WERS, 2013)

	2004	2011
Workplace with Joint Consultative Committee Coverage – private manufacturing	10%	6%
Workplace with Joint Consultative Committee Coverage – private services	5%	6%
Workplace with Joint Consultative Committee Coverage – public sector	19%	15%
European Works Councils	21%	18%

When it comes to stand-alone non-Union representations other than the above methods, there has been little change at 7 per cent for both years but in larger organizations there has been a small increase, from 6 per cent to 13 per cent.

The survey also discussed the distribution of time spent by non-Union and Union representatives in representation and the issues that were covered. Since 2004 representation on pension entitlement and performance appraisals had increased in prevalence. Though the WERS 2011 first findings (Van Wanrooy *et al*, 2013) do not attribute this to any one reason, it may be due to the changes in public sector pension entitlement and reduction in defined benefit schemes. Those without collective representation were content to raise issues with managers on their own, and for example when asked how best they were to be represented:

- 61 per cent would prefer to represent themselves for pay;
- 62 per cent would prefer to make a complaint themselves;
- 58 per cent would prefer to represent themselves with discipline matters.

The important fact from this research is that collective representation available over the period 2004 to 2011 has declined, but this has been generally of a small number, most felt in small private organizations. However it seems that employees are content with their access to representation or lack of it.

The usefulness of the WERS 2011 study

Though the WERS series does not provide information for individual companies it does enable them to see the developing trends in Employee Relations and to compare its own practice with those of others.

Organizational measures of the employment relationship

If the employment relationship is poor then it can be assumed that employees will remove themselves from the workplace, either through increased absence or by finding another job. The measures of turnover and absenteeism, therefore, can indicate the health of the employment relationship, though as always any increase in these measures cannot be said to be fully attributed to the employment relationship. It could be argued that both discipline and grievance indicate some extent of discontent or dissatisfaction and therefore measures of the number of disciplinaries or grievances can also show trends in the health of the employment relationship.

Qualitative measures

Qualitative measures provide opinions and views rather than statistical data and the employer tends to use two types of qualitative research, carrying out interviews to monitor turnover (exit interviews) and detailed questionnaires to measure engagement (attitude surveys).

The exit interview provides qualitative information, the views and opinions of employees leaving the organization and as such can be a good source of information, particularly if interviews are taken to show trends rather than viewed individually. By measuring trends the HR professional can see how the employment relationship is in different departments. Exit interviews may be useful for assessing the employees' ability to access training and available progression routes, and the effectiveness of pay and benefits as methods to retain employees. However they may not be totally reliable – some employees may express dissatisfaction others may not and they may still feel prevented from giving an honest answer by the need for a good reference. Often employers will carry out research later, after the employee has left the company, to determine those factors that have 'pushed' the employee rather than those 'pull' factors, such as pay and advancement, which have attracted employees away from the organization.

Quantitative measures

Turnover

Some turnover is needed to ensure innovation and remove ineffective employees but an excessively high turnover may indicate a problem as employees less satisfied with their job leave the organization. However it is not as simple as identifying trends and some understanding of the reason employees leave needs to be applied to the analysis. The reasons for leaving have been listed by Armstrong (2006: 380) as:

- more pay;
- better prospects;
- more security;
- more opportunity to develop skills;
- better working conditions;
- poor relationships with manager or team leader;
- poor relationship with colleagues;

- bullying or harassment;
- personal – pregnancy, illness, moving away from the area etc.

Unless employees leave for personal reasons, employees will leave their workplace when the psychological contract is breached and trust and commitment damaged, or for an improved employment relationship elsewhere. Some of the above reasons may damage the relationship and others provide the opportunity for a better relationship.

Other factors also influence turnover. The strategic decisions of a business can influence employee turnover. The lifecycle of the organization, whether it is in growth or decline, will influence the extent of turnover, as will business strategy. The employer may wish to close a site or re-deploy employees to carry out different tasks and this change may result in planned redundancies or voluntary resignations as a result of the break-up and change of teams. The employer's price strategy or differentiation strategy will have an obvious impact; if the employer has a low price strategy, its cost cutting will extend to pay, benefits and training and it is likely that employee turnover will be high. If the employer has a differentiation strategy, competing on either innovation or quality, the value placed on employees is higher and it can be assumed that the employment relationship should be better.

Redundancy may have obvious effects on the psychological contract of those employees remaining in the organization, as they can feel vulnerable, and this may therefore affect the employment relationship. But redundancy is driven by the business and therefore any increase in turnover is expected. Increased dismissals will either show an increase in misconduct as a result of a poor employment relationship, but may also show a change in management approach and applying more stringent policies. Voluntary turnover may be useful as the decision to leave may be influenced by changes in relationship with the organization that has made the employee less satisfied. However this still does not account for those that left for reasons that cannot be influenced by the employer, reasons such as the need to move area for a partner's job.

Despite the fact that the measurement of employee turnover is an inexact process it can still provide information from which the organization can assess the employment relationship. There are a number of formulae that can be used to monitor employee turnover and if measured regularly can be used to compare the extent of any retention problem and the state of the employment relationship.

The 'crude' or 'overall' turnover index measures all leavers, both those that have left involuntarily through dismissal or redundancy and those who have voluntarily left. The crude turnover index is used by the CIPD and IRS Employment Review and allows employers to benchmark their index against that for their sector or region in the same period. The crude turnover index is as follows:

$$\frac{\text{Total number of leavers over period}}{\text{Average total number employed over period}} \times 100$$

A second useful measure of turnover is the stability index. This focuses on those that remain and so looks at continuity of service. The stability index is as follows:

$$\frac{\text{Number of employees with n years' service at a given date}}{\text{Number employed n years ago}} \times 100$$

For larger employers it may be possible to use both of the measures for departments so that information can be focused on retention at department level.

Absence

Measuring absence may indicate more than the health of individual employees but may capture the absence that comes about through unengaged or demotivated employees. This link between dissatisfaction and absence is contentious and it can be argued that it is a simplistic view of absence and its causes. It assumes that demotivated employees will find ways to stay at home, and in fact there may be days when employees may take time from work pretending to be ill, for reasons as widespread as disliking their job or recovering from a hangover. However it does not account for the results of a poor employment relationship. Huczynski and Fitzpatrick (1989) in Taylor (2008: 412) listed some causes of absence in some particular cases and these included:

- general boredom with the job;
- lack of responsibility and challenge;
- forms of work-related stress;
- poor working conditions;

- work overload;
- lack of a defined workplace role;
- poor relationships with colleagues;
- poor supervision;
- frequent internal job moves.

Some of these causes can be attributed to a poor employment relationship. None of these causes are as a result of pay, the economic or transactional aspect of the employment relationship or legal rights. They relate to the social aspect of the employment relationship and the psychological contract.

Calculating absence through determining 'working days lost' in a given period, usually a year, can be used to benchmark against other companies within the sector or geographic area.

$$\frac{\text{Total number of working days lost in given period}}{\text{Total number of contracted working days over given period}} \times 100$$

Conclusion

Often employers can be inward-looking, and this focuses their attention on factors that influence the employment relationship that are outside their control. National measurements of the employment relationship give employers a useful perspective. However, measuring the employment relationship remains difficult and the tools available to the HR professional do not measure the relationship alone but are influenced by other factors. However we do need to survey employees and gain an understanding of their views and this chapter has examined how to design our own surveys. Engagement, absence and turnover measures however will give an indication and can be benchmarked against the average in the sector or geographic area. They can also be used to indicate the impact of techniques used to improve engagement and the employment relationship so that we can make improvements.

Just before we take a look at the future of Employee Relations, evaluating the environment that influences it and how this might affect us as HR professionals, we finish with a case study and diagnostic questionnaire. The case study below describes how research into absence in the Police Force reflected the state of the employment relationship as well as the health of police officers.

CASE STUDY   Absence in the Police Force

Research was carried out by the Institute of Employment Studies for the Health and Safety Executive and Home Office to assess current absence management practices in the Police Force. The report recognized that absence management was more than policy and practice but that '*successful absence management fundamentally depends on addressing wider organisational and management factors such as the culture of the organisation, their approach to well-being at work, communication skills and the ability of line managers to competently deliver policy*' (IES, 2007: 6) and therefore while some of it related to absence management processes, some information was relevant to the employment relationship.

The research was carried out in seven police forces, a mix of rural and urban forces, using focus groups, questionnaires, face-to-face and telephone interviews. Forty-two interviews of senior managers were completed, 280 participants of focus groups were questioned, including Line Managers, Trade Union representatives, Police staff and officers and some returners from long-term sickness. Telephone interviews were completed with eight employees on long-term sickness during the period of the research.

The Police Force is working towards measuring average hours lost to sickness per officer per shift pattern hours and forces that have a Duty Management System have greater ease in calculating this. However there is a lack of consistent approaches to absence monitoring between forces. Due to the inconsistency of measurement forces did not benchmark against other forces but did use the Home Office annual national target absence figures.

The research suggested that few employees took time off work for non-health issues, and in fact some police officers thought that employees would come in while sick to maintain a good sick record and because of the good working environment. When sickness absence was taken for an illness or injury it was suggested that the factors that caused the decision to be absent was often complex, involving the extent of illness or injury along with work and personal issues.

It was recognized that workplace issues did impact upon absence. The physical nature of the job at times led to injury or illness. Work pressures, increased bureaucracy, performance targets, limited resources and inflexible shift patterns were all cited. Some officers felt undervalued, especially if they were involved in reactive work. At times absence was thought to be as a result of dissatisfaction.

> *You could never prove it, but you know it, because you'll overhear throw-away remarks from people. You know, something may have happened work-wise that just hasn't been to their liking. Next thing you know is: some people will just go off sick, throw in the towel and go off sick. I wonder if they see it as a way of getting back at the organization.*
>
> (Staff) (IES, 2007: 61)

The role of the Line Manager was vital in the management of absence, both for long-term absence and facilitating return to work and forces experiencing organizational change especially in relation to resources put an extra strain on the employment relationship.

The Police Force had a number of strategies that would decrease absence and simultaneously improve the employment relationship. Special leave allowed employees to take time off to deal with emergencies at home. Flexible working had been a successful tool, allowing employees to manage home commitments effectively and a more flexible approach to shifts has also been viewed in a positive light by employees. There were also a range of health and well-being initiatives, for example gym membership discounts and mobile health checks. However the closure of police canteens meant that it was difficult to access hot food when on shift work.

In conclusion the Police Force is experiencing the challenges of reduced funding and increasing demand, and it was clear that the issues surrounding these had influenced the employment relationship. There were some interventions that improved the relationship, but the perception of their relationship with manage-ment and the organization was important and impacted on the absence in the Police Force.

DIAGNOSTIC QUESTIONNAIRE Measuring the employment relationship

This questionnaire is for you to assess your own satisfaction with your relationship with your direct Line Manager and the organization. It may be used in some cases as a discussion in smaller teams but is an informal tool rather than a standardized test.

		Always	Never	Sometimes	Often
1	I can talk to my Line Manager	☐	☐	☐	☐
2	I feel I am in control of how I do my work	☐	☐	☐	☐
3	My Line Manager appreciates me when I do a good job	☐	☐	☐	☐
4	My Line Manager keeps me up to date.	☐	☐	☐	☐
5	I can influence decisions about my work.	☐	☐	☐	☐
6	I feel I am listened to by my Line Manager.	☐	☐	☐	☐
7	I like working for my Line Manager.	☐	☐	☐	☐
8	I can tell my Line Manager if I am overloaded.	☐	☐	☐	☐
9	My Line Manager treats me fairly.	☐	☐	☐	☐
10	I feel my Line Manager stands up for me.	☐	☐	☐	☐
11	I am committed to the organization.	☐	☐	☐	☐
12	I am content with the level of training.	☐	☐	☐	☐

	Always	Never	Sometimes	Often
13 I think of leaving the organization.	☐	☐	☐	☐
14 I am well informed about what is going on.	☐	☐	☐	☐
15 I feel treated fairly by my organization.	☐	☐	☐	☐
16 I feel my job is secure.	☐	☐	☐	☐
17 I feel senior managers have trust and confidence in me	☐	☐	☐	☐
18 I have trust and confidence in senior management.	☐	☐	☐	☐
19 I am content with my level of pay for what I do.	☐	☐	☐	☐
20 I do my best for the organization.	☐	☐	☐	☐

Scoring

For each 'never' mark you score 0, for each 'sometimes' mark score 1, for each 'often' mark score 2 and for each 'always' mark score 3. Add up your scores for questions 1–10 and questions 11–20 separately.

Scores for Q1–10 (Line Manager)

If you score between 20–30 this means that you have a majority of 'always' answers and have an excellent relationship with your Line Manager. You clearly know what is going on, can make decisions over your work and feel you have a voice. Your interactions with your Line Manager are positive and in general you feel that decisions are just – particularly in terms of interactional justice.

If you score between 10–20 you have a majority of 'often' answers and you have a good relationship with your Line Manager. There is scope to improve but you are generally satisfied with the relationship and it is likely that you are respected and trusted by your Line Manager.

If you score 0–10 you have a majority of 'sometimes' answers and could improve your relationship with your Line Manager. You can feel disengaged and demotivated, and your Line Manager may not communicate with you, either listening to you or keeping you up to date. You have little power over what or how you do things. You may find decisions go against you, but your Line Manager may not have built a good enough relationship with you to help you accept these reasonably well.

Scores for Q11–20 (The Organization)
If you score 20–30 you have a majority of 'always' answers and have an excellent relationship with your employer. This relationship works both ways as you give commitment and do your best. The employment relationship is best in smaller organizations and ones where there are similar values, and you may find that this is your experience. It is unlikely that you had a low score for your Line Manager relationship as this is your direct link with your employer.

If you score 10–20 you have a majority of 'often' answers and have a good relationship with the organization. You feel valued in terms of the way you are treated, with more than a transactional relationship. You are reasonably content with your rewards for effort in terms of the training and pay you receive. You are more likely to score highly if you work for a small organization or have shared values with your organization.

If you score 0–10 you have a majority of 'sometimes' answers and you have a serious issue with your organization. Your response suggests that occasionally you are committed but that you may feel that there are some promises that have been broken (the psychological contract may have been breached) or that you are feeling used. You may feel that procedures are unfair or unclear and decisions made may seem unjust. An employer does not get the most out of the employee if this is the level of engagement, and the employee does not enjoy the experience of work. It becomes a transactional relationship. As with all relationships there are bad patches and it is necessary to determine at what point the relationship has broken down.

Conclusion

Summary

Throughout this book we have seen the importance of Employee Relations and how to practise it effectively. We have attempted to explain how Employee Relations is relevant today, its role in supporting business to improve performance, and the need for a strategic view. We have enabled HR professionals to implement the different aspects of Employee Relations and discussed the skills needed by modern HR professionals working with employees and supporting Line Managers.

The fact that there are many organizations influencing Employee Relations (national organizations such as ACAS and the CBI, and international ones such as the International Labour Organization) indicates that Employee Relations is not carried out within companies in isolation. The environment in which the employer exists influences the employment relationship. We conclude by examining the environment and the changes that may affect Employee Relations.

UK politics and the law

In the past, political policy has had a profound effect on Employee Relations. For example, the Conservative Government from 1979–97 reduced the power of the Trade Unions, and the Coalition Government has more recently reduced employment regulation and employee rights. Labour Governments have not reversed this trend towards support of the employer, though they are more supportive of Trade Unions. We as HR professionals may have had to implement these laws or have seen them applied – laws which have, for example, restricted the ability of Trade Unions to strike, affected the way discipline procedures are carried out, and influenced how multinational corporations communicate and involve their staff.

Government policy implemented through law, defines the boundaries of the employment relationship, ensuring the employees have protection from unscrupulous employers whilst the employer can run a profitable business without excessive regulation. We feel the impact of law as an HR professional advising the employer on how to manage the changes in law, but will also as employees make sure that our rights are protected if we seek, for example, maternity leave or request flexible working. It is a balance between employer and employee and both sides can feel that the balance of regulation is unfair.

Since 2008 the UK has been struggling to recover from the economic downturn, and it is projected that though it is unlikely that another deep recession is imminent this economic challenge will continue. It is in this context that any review of future trends and changes to Employee Relations must be made, as Government policy will attempt to build a stronger economy, with stronger businesses more willing to invest in new staff if the legal restrictions placed on them are less onerous. It is therefore likely that the rights of employees will be eroded as the needs of business are of greater importance for the economy.

The changing workforce

The workplace has changed: more of the workforce now has a degree or higher level qualification (CIPD, 2013) and this has supported the increase of knowledge-based services (and a resultant reduction in the manufacturing industry). It is difficult to interpret how this change may affect Employee Relations in the future but a more educated workforce may in the long-term have greater expectations of their career and pay – at the moment, the primary demand of the workforce is to gain and retain employment. They may also expect a greater voice and be less likely to join a Trade Union. We may need to develop and foster voice mechanisms to meet this change.

Those entering the labour market have been badly hit by the recession, as those seeking their first jobs are a greater risk to employers than those with a track record of employment. The impact on the young is difficult to project into the future, but it may be that this also will have pushed young people towards improving their education or into lower paid or part-time jobs with little future, such as cleaning or personal care, where the growth in jobs have been. It is these employees that will be most vulnerable to job insecurity in the future, moving from employer to employer and in 2008 the Commission on Vulnerable Work, established by the TUC, reported on the increasing number of vulnerable workers. Since then the Agency Workers Regulations (2010) have helped to protect agency workers but also the date when employees can seek legal protection against unfair dismissal has been extended to two years. Time is needed to assess the impact on this for those more vulnerable employees and the role of Trade Unions will have to support this type of employee. We as HR professionals need to ensure we remember our duty to work within ethical and legal boundaries.

The age profile of workers has also changed with fewer young employees, as previously explained, and more employees over 50 (CIPD, 2013). The reasons are various, including the inability for older people to afford to retire, changes in automatic retirement at 65 and demographic changes increasing the number of older people in the population. However this impacts employers as they may need to retain and retrain older employees and we will need to look to methods to engage these workers and develop their new skills.

There have been such radical changes in women's working lives that it is difficult to envisage much more change in the future. Women make up a large proportion of the workforce, and maternity legislation supports their return to work after the birth of children. Changes in access to leave for parents may lead to fathers taking more paternity leave after the birth of their child. However it is difficult to predict how these changes will be viewed by parents and whether they will have any impact on women's chances of gaining leadership positions or reduce the gender pay gap – the two remaining inequalities for women.

Technology

The development of digital technology has revolutionized working life and enabled the wide range of working patterns that we see today. Employees do not just attend work as full-time employees working 9–5 but with customers demanding access to services 24/7, technology in particular has enabled employees to meet this demand. For example technological developments have meant that we can now see local supermarkets open throughout the night, orders made overnight packed and sent the next morning, in a world where demand can be met instantly and where increasingly the same is expected of employees. Many employees are able to use technology to work from home, attending telephone or video conferences, accessing training sessions through webinars and being part of a virtual team, with team members situated across the globe. They check emails and make appointments at all times of day and night. Cloud technology means that documents can be accessed from tablets, laptops, desktops or phones from different venues, different countries and different users so virtual teams can work on projects from different sites around the clock.

For HR professionals managing issues of grievance and discipline this may at times become more challenging as the boundary between private home life and working life becomes blurred. We may find that engaging employees who work in a virtual team and have little physical contact with other employees could be an interesting challenge. Many HR professionals have global responsibilities and have to apply varied employment legislation dependent on the country that the employee works in.

Role of Trade Unions

In the UK the impact of the Trade Union movement in the workplace has been in slow decline. Only 21 per cent of employers recognize a Trade Union and Union membership has dropped to 30 per cent (WERS, Van Wanrooy *et al*, 2013). This continues a steady trend away from Trade Union representation. However this does not mean that the Trade Union movement fails to influence Government policy; on the contrary, the TUC has an active presence.

Internationally the Trade Union movement is developing innovative approaches to protecting employees in multinational corporations, using international framework agreements. This is a particularly important development as Global Union Federations seek to protect employees of a company with a globally fragmented supply chain – protecting employees of the one multinational corporation working in different countries. Most of the international framework agreements are based on the international labour standards established by the International Labour Organization, but top-down bilateral agreements are based more on employee protection than employee voice (Thomas, 2011). The agreements have the potential to evolve to become more than a bilateral code of conduct to support employer voice globally, but this will require circumstances that allow Global Union Federations to push for this and multinational corporations to view this as in their interests.

For HR professionals we may find we work with Trade Unions less often and we will need to maintain our skills in this field. We may find that partnership working with Trade Unions increases, and those without Trade Unions may seek to develop strong communication methods with individual employees to build a strong employment relationship. We may also need to look at other ways to support employee voice and resolve individual disputes.

Involvement, participation and voice

The future of employee involvement, participation and voice is difficult to predict because it is influenced by so many different factors. It could be argued that the continued economic crisis has put a hold on developments in EIP, yet the involvement and participation of employees may be the critical factor in innovation and creativity – to enhance the future of our companies. We as HR professionals have not had employee involvement schemes at the top of our list – we have been more concerned with redundancies and pay freezes.

In the UK our liberal society values such as the contribution of the individual and of freedom and justice prevail and run alongside a capitalist economy and the need for profitable business. In the 1970s the UK established equality legislation far advanced of its European neighbours yet simultaneously the UK fostered a strong small business sector. European legislation, such as the ICE Regulations and the use of European Works Councils, has also influenced the development of employee involvement and voice, yet the threat of redundancy may stifle any employee voice in our present time of economic crisis.

Conclusion – the future role of Employee Relations

So what is the future of Employee Relations? The CIPD (2013) describes HR as '*delivering organizational capability and performance*' and argues for HR professionals to have their place on the top table. HR has a place to ensure the future profitability of the company, to gain respect and prestige, to have a powerful influence, securing our position as a profession and our reputation. Without the profitability of companies we will not pull ourselves out of this economic quagmire and provide the salaries to help our employees pull themselves out of the debt that they are in. The capitalist economy supports us all in the end. And this is a convincing argument.

But in the UK our past and our values need not be forgotten in the search for profit. After a long struggle the workforce was able to speak collectively as each individual voice was too weak. Now we look forward to, more often, confident individual relationships with our employees, yet this does not mean that the power in this relationship is balanced. Our role is to support Line Managers to build good employment relationships with our employees. We know we need to develop good relationships to get the best out of our employees, to build loyalty and commitment that is invaluable. And along with any relationship, we need to support employees to contribute to the future of their company, to their future, building on their skills so that they are as able as possible to do this. Then these stakeholders will contribute to the profit that we all seek.

REFERENCES

Abbott, B, Heery, E and Williams, S (2012) Civil Society Organizations and the Exercise of Power in the Employment Relationship, *Employee Relations*, **34** (1), pp 91–107

Adair, J and Thomas, N (2004) *The Concise Adair on Creativity and Innovation*, Thorogood, London

Adams, J S (1965) Inequity in social exchange, in L Berkowitz ed, *Advances in Experimental Social Psychology*, vol 2, pp 267–99, Academic, New York

ACAS (2003) [accessed 26 December 2012] Code of Practice 2: Disclosure of Information to Trade Unions for Collective Bargaining Purposes [Online] http://www.acas.org.uk/media/pdf/2/q/CP02_1.pdf

ACAS (2008) [accessed 19 January 2013] Mediation: An Employer's Guide. [Online] http://www.acas.org.uk/media/pdf/f/3/Joint_ACAS_CIPDMediation_guide_SEPT2008.pdf

ACAS (2009a) Managing Conflict at Work [Online] http://www.acas.co.uk/CHttpHandler.ashx?id=960&p=0

ACAS (2009b) Employee Communications and Consultation [Online] http://www.acas.org.uk/index.aspx?articleid=663

ACAS (2009c) [accessed 26 December 2012] Code of Practice 1: Discipline and Grievance Procedures [Online] http://www.acas.org.uk/media/pdf/k/b/Acas_Code_of_Practice_1_on_disciplinary_and_grievance_procedures-accessible-version-Jul-2012.pdf

ACAS (2009d) [accessed 26 December 2012] Trade Union Representation in the Workplace [Online] http://www.acas.org.uk/CHttpHandler.ashx?id=2307&p=0

ACAS (2010) [accessed 26 December 2012] Code of Practice 3: Time Off for Trade Union Duties and Activities [Online] http://www.acas.org.uk/media/pdf/n/k/Acas_Code_of_Practice_Part-3-accessible-version-July-2011.pdf

ACAS (2011) [accessed 11 December 2012] Discipline and Grievances at Work [Online] http://www.acas.org.uk/media/pdf/s/o/Acas-Guide-on-discipline-and-grievances_at_work_(April_11)-accessible-version-may-2012.pdf

ACAS (2012) [accessed 27 October 2012] Redundancy Handling [Online] http://www.acas.org.uk/index.aspx?articleid=747

Agency Workers Regulations 2010, HMSO, London

Aidt, T and Tzannatos, Z (2008) Trade Unions, collective bargaining and macroeconomic performance: a review, *Industrial Relations Review*, **39** (4), pp 258–95

Airbus UK Ltd v Webb, Court of Appeal (2008) EWCA Civ 49

Albrecht, K (2013) [accessed 22 July 2013] Employee Quality of Working Life Survey [Online] https://www.karlalbrecht.com/downloads/Albrecht-EQWLS-Survey-Qnr.pdf

Amazon (2011) [accessed 23 July 2013] Amazon Investor Relations [Online] http://phx.corporate-ir.net/phoenix.zhtml?c=97664&p=irol-irhome

Amazon (2012) [accessed 23 July 2013] Amazon.com Annual Report [Online] http://phx.corporate-ir.net/phoenix.zhtml?c=97664&p=irol-reportsAnnual

Appelbaum, S, Abdallah, C and Shapiro, B (1999) The self-directed team: a conflict resolution analysis, *Team Performance Management*, 5 (2), pp 60–77

Armstrong (2006) *A Handbook of Human Resource Management Practice*, 10th edn, Kogan Page, London

Aylott, E (2014) *HR Fundamentals: Employment Law*, Kogan Page, London

Ayub and Kahn (2011) The moderating role of social attitudes in the relationship between diversity and conflict, *Current Topics in Management*, 15, pp 13–40

Badke-Schaub, P, Goldschmidt, G and Meijer, M (2010) How does cognitive conflict in design teams support the development of creative ideas? *Creativity and Innovation Management*, 19 (2), pp 119–233

Barry, M and May, R (2004) New employee representation: legal developments and New Zealand unions, *Employee Relations*, 26 (2), pp 203–23

Basu, D and Miroshnik, V (1999) Strategic human resource management of Japanese multinationals – a case study of Japanese multinational companies in the UK, *Journal of Management Development*, 18 (9), pp 714–32

BBC (2012) [accessed 9 November 2012] Hyundai union members vote in favour of new wage deal [Online] http://www.bbc.co.uk/news/business-19472853

Behrend, H (1988) The wage–work bargain, *Managerial and Decision Economics*, 9, pp 51–57

Bies, R (2001) Interactional (in)justice: the sacred and the profane, in Greenberg, J and Cropanzano, R (eds) *Advances in Organizational Justice*, Stanford University Press, Palo Alto, CA

BIS (1992) [accessed 26 December 2012] Picketing Code of Practice [Online] http://www.bis.gov.uk/assets/biscore/employment-matters/docs/P/96-618-picketing.pdf

BIS (2005) Code of Practice: Industrial action ballots and notice to employers [Online] http://www.bis.gov.uk/files/file18013.pdf

Blau, P (1964) *Exchange and Power in Social Life*, Wiley, New York

Brahm, E, Conflict stages, in G Burgess and H Burgess (eds) *Beyond Intractability*, Conflict Information Consortium, University of Colorado, Boulder. Posted: September 2003 http://www.beyondintractability.org/bi-essay/conflict-stages

British Homes Stores v Burchell (1980) ICR 303, EAT

Bryson, A, Forth, J and Kirby, S (2005) High-involvement management practices, trade union representation and workplace performance in Britain, *Scottish Journal of Political Economy*, 52 (3), pp 451–91

Bryson, A, Forth, J and George, A (2012) Workplace social dialogue in Europe: an analysis of the European Company Survey 2009, *Eurofound*, Dublin, Ireland

Bureau of Labor Statistics (2012) [accessed 17 March 2013] Economic News Release: Union Members Summary [Online] http://www.bls.gov/news.release/union2.nr0.htm

Bush, A and Folger, J (1994) *The Promise of Mediation: Responding to conflict through empowerment and recognition*, Jossey-Bass Publishers, San Francisco, CA

Business Europe (2012) [accessed 27 October 2012] [Online] http://www.businesseurope.eu/Content/Default.asp

CAB (2013) [accessed 26 July 2013] Citizens Advice: About Us [Online] http://www.citizensadvice.org.uk/index/aboutus.htm

Caglar, D, Kesteloo, M and Kleiner, A (2012) [accessed 16 March 2013] How Ikea Reassembled Its Growth Strategy, *Strategy+Business* [Online] http://www.strategy-business.com/article/00111

Cappelli, P and Chauvin, K (1991) A test of an efficiency model of grievance activity, *Industrial and Labor Relations Review*, 45, pp 3–13

CBI (2011) [accessed 6 November 2012] Thinking Positively: the 21st century employment relationship [Online] http://content.yudu.com/A1sg86/CBI-Thinkingpositive/resources/index.htm?referrerUrl=

CBI (2012) [accessed 16 March 2013] *About the CBI* [Online] http://www.cbi.org.uk/about-the-cbi/

CIPD (2008) *Managing Conflict at Work: A guide for line managers*, CIPD, London

CIPD (2011) [accessed 17 January 2013] Conflict Management [Online] http://www.cipd.co.uk/binaries/5461_Conflict_manage_SR_WEB.pdf

CIPD (2012a) [accessed 13 October 2012] The Psychological Contract [Online] www.cipd.co.uk/hr-resources/factsheets/psychological-contract.aspx

CIPD (2012b) [accessed 6 November 2012] CIPD and the HR Profession [Online] http://www.cipd.co.uk/cipd-hr-profession/

CIPD (2012c) [accessed 6 November 2012] CIPD Code of Professional Conduct [Online] http://www.cipd.co.uk/NR/rdonlyres/476C73A1-FBCD-4D08-A50E-2ACD31CF8E94/0/5740CodeofConduct.pdf

CIPD (2012d) *Managing Employee Relations in Difficult Times*, CIPD, London

CIPD (2012e) [accessed 26 July 2013] HR Professions Map [Online] http://www.cipd.co.uk/cipd-hr-profession/hr-profession-map/hr-profession-map-download.aspx

CIPD (2012f) [Accessed 5 January 2013] Employee Engagement [Online] http://www.cipd.co.uk/hr-resources/factsheets/employee-engagement.aspx

CIPD (2013) [accessed 21 July 2013] Megatrends: The trends shaping work and working lives [Online] http://www.cipd.co.uk/binaries/6251%20Megatrends%20%28WEB%29.pdf

Circle (2011) [accessed 16 March 2013] Our Partnership [Online] http://www.circlepartnership.co.uk/about-circle/our-partnership

Civil Mediation Council (2009) [accessed 26 July 2013] Civil Mediation Council [Online] http://www.civilmediation.org/

Coca-Cola (2010) [accessed 2 November 2012] About us [Online] http://www.coca-cola.co.uk/about-us/coca-cola-mission-vision-statement.html

Colquitt, J A, Conlon, D E, Wesson, M J, Porter, C and Ng, K Y (2001) Justice at the Millennium: A meta-analytic review of 25 years of organizational justice, *Journal of Applied Psychology*, **86**, pp 425–45

Dasgupta, S, Suar, D and Singh, S (2013) Impact of managerial communication styles on employees' attitudes and behaviours, *Employee Relations: The International Journal*, **35** (2), pp 173–99

Davidson v Kent Meters Ltd (1975) IRLR 145

Den Hartog, D N and Verburg, R M (2004) High performance work systems, organisational culture and firm effectiveness, *Human Resource Management Journal*, **14** (1), pp 55–78

Denco v Joinson [1991] ICR 172, IRLR 63

Dibben, K, Klerck, G and Wood, G (2011) *Employment Relations: A critical and international approach*, CIPD, London

Diosynth Ltd v Thomson, Court of Session (Inner House), (2006) IRLR 284

Dulac, T, Coyle-Shapiro, J, Henderson, D and Wayne, S (2008) Not all responses to breach are the same: the interconnection of social exchange and psychological contract processes in organizations, *Academy of Management Journal*, **51** (6), pp 1079–98

Dundon, T and Gollan, P (2007) The re-conceptualising voice in the non-union workplace, *International Journal of Human Resource Management*, **18** (7), pp 1182–98

EIRR (1993) The Hoover Affair and social dumping, *European Industrial Relations Review*, **230**, **pp 14–19**

Employment Act 2002, HMSO, London

Employment Relations Act 1999, HMSO, London

Employment Rights Act 1996, HMSO, London

Equality Act 2010, HMSO, London

ETUC (2011) [accessed 27 October 2012] *Our Aims* [Online] http://www.etuc.org/r/2

European Works Council Directive 2009/38/EC 6 May 2009

Farnham, D (2000) *Employee Relations in Context*, CIPD, London

Fayol, H (1949) *General and Industrial Administration*, Pitman, London

Ferris, G and Kacmar, K (1992) Perceptions of organizational politics, *Journal of Management*, **18**, pp 93–116

Fisher, C and Lovell, A (2009) *Business Ethics and Values: Individual, corporate and international perspectives*, 3rd edn, Pearson Education, Harlow

Forbes (2012) [accessed 16 March 2013] The World's Most Innovative Companies [Online] http://www.forbes.com/innovative-companies/list/

Forman, A S and Watkins, E E (2009) Here are 10 cases of sabotage that harmed – or attempted to harm – some high-profile companies, *Human Resource Executive* [Online] http://www.hreonline.com/HRE/story.jsp?storyId=225549614&query=sabotage

FT (2013) [Accessed 23 July 2013] Amazon Unpacked [Online] http://www.ft.com/cms/s/2/ed6a985c-70bd-11e2-85d0-00144feab49a.html#slide0

Gaitan, R and Kleiner, B (1999) How to conduct mediation effectively, *Equal Opportunities International*, 18 (5), pp 69–73

Gate Gourmet London Ltd v Transport and General Workers' Union and others (2005) IRLR 881, QBD

Gennard, J and Judge, G (2010) *Employee Relations*, 5th ed, CIPD, London

Gibbons, M (2007) *Better Dispute Resolution: A review of employment dispute resolution in Great Britain*, Department of Trade and Industry, London

GKN (2012) [accessed 30 December 2012] *About Us* [Online] http://www.gkn.com/aboutus/Pages/default.aspx

Gordon, M E and Bowlby, R L (1989) Reactance and intentionality attributions as determinants of the intent to file a grievance, *Personnel Psychology*, 42, pp 309–29

W A Gould (Pearmak) Ltd v McConnell and anor [1995] IRLR 516

Greer, C and Stephens, G (1996) Employee relations issues in US companies in mexico, *California Management Review*, 38 (3), pp 121–37

Guest, D and Conway, N (2002) *Pressure at Work and the Psychological Contract*, research report, Chartered Institute of Personnel and Development, London

Gumbrell-McCormick, R and Hyman, R (2006), *Industrial Relations Journal*, 37 (5), pp 473–91

Handel, M J and Levine, D (2004) Editors' introduction: the effects of new work practices on workers, *Industrial Relations*, 43 (1), pp 1–43

Heery, E, Abbott, B and Williams, S (2012) The involvement of civil society organisations in British industrial relations: extent, origins, significance, *British Journal of Industrial Relations*, 50 (1), pp 47–72

Herman, R, Gioia, J and Chalkley, T (1998) Making work meaningful, *Futurist*, 32 (9), pp 24–38

Hock, M (2012) [accessed 6 November 2012] New estimate puts gulf oil leak at 205 million gallons, PBS NewsHour, MacNeil /Lehrer Productions [Online] http://www.pbs.org/newshour/rundown/2010/08/new-estimate-puts-oil-leak-at-49-million-barrels.html

Hotson v Wishbech Conservative Club (1984) ICT 859 EAT

House of Commons Culture, Media and Sport Committee (2012) *News International and Phone-hacking Eleventh Report of Session 2010–2012* (HC 903–1), HMSO, London

HSBC Group (2012a) [accessed 31 October 2012] *International Management* [Online] http://www.hsbc.com/1/2/careers/im/about

HSBC Group (2012b)[accessed 31 October 2012] HSBC International Careers: International management programme [Online] http://www.hsbc.com/1/ PA_esf-ca-app-content/content/assets/careers/grads_im/2011/111115_im_ brochure.pdf

Hunter v Timber Components (Ltd) [2009] UKEAT 0025/09

Hyman, J and Mason, B (1995) *Managing Employee Involvement and Participation*, Sage, London

Information and Consultation of Employees Regulations 2004, HMSO, London

Institute for Employment Studies (2007) *Managing Sickness Absence in the Police Service: A review of current practices*, HSE, London

International Labour Organization (2006) [accessed 13 October 2012] Report V (1) The Employment Relationship, International Labour Conference, 95th Session [Online] http://www.ilo.org/public/english/standards/relm/ilc/ilc95/pdf/ rep-v-1.pdf

International Labour Organization (2012a) *The World of Work Report 2012: Better jobs for a better economy*, International Labour Office, International Institute for Labour Studies, Geneva

International Labour Organization (2012b) [accessed 31 October 2012] C087 – Freedom of Association and Protection of the Right to Organise Convention, 1948 (No. 87) [Online] http://www.ilo.org/dyn/normlex/ en/f?p=NORMLEXPUB:11310:0::NO:11310:P11310_INSTRUMENT_ ID:312232:NO

International Labour Organization (2012c) [accessed 31 October 2012] *Ratifications of C098 – Right to Organise and Collective Bargaining Convention, 1949 (No. 98)* [Online] http://www.ilo.org/dyn/normlex/en/f? p=NORMLEXPUB:11300:0::NO:11300:P11300_INSTRUMENT_ID:312243:NO

International Trade Union Confederation (2006) [accessed 27 October 2012] *The Programme of the ITUC* [Online] http://www.ituc-csi.org/IMG/pdf/ Programme_of_the_ITUC.pdf

International Transport Workers Federation (2012) [accessed 27 October 2012] Union pressure wins removal of strike ban [Online] http://www.itfglobal.org/ news-online/index.cfm/newsdetail/8072

IPA and Tomorrow's Company (2012) [accessed 5 January 2012] Releasing Voice for Sustainable Business Success [Online] http://www.engageforsuccess.org/ ideas-tools/releasing-voice-for-sustainable-business-success/

James, P (1995) US Labor Law reform: a note on the Dunlop Debate, *Employee Relations*, **17** (6), pp 43–51

Jameson, H (2011) [accessed 20 November 2012] Engaging and Involving Employees at Circle, London, IPA [Online] http://www.ipa-involve.com/ resources/publications/engaging-and-involving-employees/

Jehn, K (1997) A qualitative analysis of conflict types and dimensions in organizational groups, *Administrative Science Quarterly*, **42**, pp 530–57

Jehn, K A and Mannix, E (2001) The dynamic nature of conflict: a longitudinal study of intragroup conflict and group performance, *Academy of Management Journal*, **44**, pp 238–51

Kamprad, I (2007) [accessed 16 March 2013] The Testament of a Furniture Dealer: A little IKEA dictionary, Inter IKEA systems B.V [Online] http://www.emu.dk/erhverv/merkantil_caseeksamen/doc/ikea/english_testament_2007.pdf

Kanungo, R N and Mendonca, M (1996) *Ethical Dimensions of Leadership*, Sage, London

Kersley, B, Alpin, C, Forth, J, Bryson, A, Bewley, H, Dix, G and Oxenbridge, S (2005) *Inside the Workplace: First findings from the 2004 Workplace Employment Relations Survey (WERS 2004)*, Department of Trade and Industry, London

Kochan, T and Barocci, T (1985) *Human Resource Management and Industrial Relations*, Little Brown, Boston

Kollewe, J (2012) [accessed 28 Oct 2012] Unemployment falls to 15-month low, *Guardian.co.uk* [Online] http://www.guardian.co.uk/business/2012/oct/17/uk-unemployment-falls-lowest-ons

Latreille, P (2010) Mediation at Work: Of success, failure and fragility, ACAS, London [Online] http://www.acas.org.uk/media/pdf/1/4/Mediation_at_work_of_success-failure_and_fragility-accessible-version-may-2012.pdf

Leventhal, G S (1980) What should be done with equity theory? in Gergen, K J, Greenberg, M S and Willis, R H (eds), *Social Exchange: Advances in theory and research*, pp 27–55, Plenum, New York, NY

Linfood Cash and Carry Ltd v Thomson and anor (1989) ICR 518

London Borough of Waltham Forest vs. Omilaju [2004] EWCA Civ 1493

London Underground v Ferenc-Batchelor and *Harding v London Underground Ltd* (2003) ICR 656, EAT

Low Pay Commission (2013) [accessed 12 June 2013] National Minimum Wage: Low Pay Commission Report [Online] http://www.lowpay.gov.uk/lowpay/report/pdf/9305-BIS-Low_Pay-Accessible6.pdf

Luckhurst, D and Jameson, H (2011) *Partnership Working: A practitioner's guide*, IPA, London

MacNeil, I R (1974) The many futures of contracts, *Southern California Law Review*, **47**, pp 691–816

MacNeil, I R (1985) Relational contract: what we do and what we do not know, *Wisconsin Law Review*, **3**, pp 483–525

Mansfield Hosiery Mills Ltd v Bromley EAT (1977) IRLR 301

Marchington, M and Kynighoe, A (2012) The dynamics of employee involvement and participation during turbulent times, *International Journal of Human Resource Management*, **23** (16), pp 3336–54

Maslow, A (1987) *Motivation and Personality*, 3rd edn, Addison-Wesley, NY

Maternity and Parental Leave Regulations 1999, HMSO, London

McDermott, C and Westcott, R (1996) *Fiscal Reform that Works*, International Monetary Fund, Washington

McKenna, E (2006) *Business Psychology and Organizational Behaviour*, Psychology Press, NY

Melé, D (2012) The firm as a community of persons: a pillar of humanistic business ethos, *Journal of Business Ethics*, **106** (1), pp 89–101

Midland Plastics v Till and other (1983) ICR 118, EAT

Miller v Executor of John C Graham (1978) IRLR 309

Ministry of Justice (2012) [accessed 26 July 2013] Employment Tribunal and EAT Statistics, 2011–2012 [Online] https://www.gov.uk/government/uploads/system/uploads/attachment_data/file/218497/employment-trib-stats-april-march-2011-12.pdf

Mullins, L (2001) *Hospitality Management and Organisational Behaviour*, Pearson Education, Harlow

Mullins, L (2005) *Management and Organisational Behaviour*, 9th ed, Prentice Hall/Financial Times, Harlow

National Minimum Wage Act (1998) HMSO, London

Nergaard, K (2011) [accessed 27 October 2012] Hospitals ordered to reduce part-time work [Online] http://www.eurofound.europa.eu/eiro/2011/03/articles/no1103019i.htm

NIKEINC (2011a) [accessed 16 March 2013] About NIKE [Online] http://nikeinc.com/pages/about-nike-inc

NIKEINC (2011b) [accessed 16 March 2013] Locations [Online] http://nikeinc.com/pages/locations

Ocado (2012) [accessed 2 November 2012] Mission Statement [Online] http://www.ocado.com/careers/jump.do?jt=mission-statement

OECD (2010) [accessed at 16 March 2013] Statistics on Trade Union Density, OECD, Paris [Online] http://stats.oecd.org/Index.aspx?DataSetCode=UN_DEN

Office for National Statistics (2012) [accessed 9 November 2012] Labour Market Statistics: Statistical Bulletin [Online] http://www.ons.gov.uk/ons/dcp171778_279723.pdf

Part-time Workers (Prevention of Less Favourable Treatment) Regulations 2000 HMSO, London

Paulus, P (2000) Groups, teams and creativity: the creativity potential of idea-generating groups, *Applied Psychology*, **49** (2), pp 237–62

Pedersini, R (2003) [accessed 30 December 2012] Industrial Relations in the Automotive Sector [Online] http://www.eurofound.europa.eu/eiro/2003/12/study/tn0312101s.htm

People Management (2011) [accessed 14 November 2012] Knowledge Management: In perspective [Online] http://www.peoplemanagement.co.uk/pm/articles/2011/06/knowledge-management-in-perspective.htm

People Management (2003) Professional Standards Research: the psychological contract [Online] http://www.peoplemanagement.co.uk/pm/articles/2003/07/9215.htm

Personnel Today (2005) [accessed 14 November 2012] British Gas asks outgoing UK staff to train successors in India [Online] http://www.personneltoday.com/Articles/12/08/2005/31179/British-Gas-asks-outgoing-UK-staff-to-train-successors-in.htm

Pfeffer, J (1994) *Competitive Advantage Through People: Unleashing the power of the workforce*, Harvard Business Press, Boston, MA

Porter (1985) *Competitive Advantage*, Free Press, New York

Porter v Magill (2002) 2 AC 357

Pruitt, D G and Kim, S H (2004) *Social Conflict: Escalation, stalemate and settlement*, McGraw-Hill, Boston

Raven, B and French, J Jr (1959) The bases of social power, in D Cartwright (ed), *Studies in Social Power* (pp 150–67), Institute for Social Research, Ann Arbor, MI

Recruitment and Employment Confederation (2012) [accessed 31 October 2012] Current News: Flexible work drives record employment [Online] http://www.rec.uk.com/press/news/2219

Redman, T and Wilkinson, A (2009) *Contemporary Human Resource Management: Text and cases*, Financial Times / Prentice Hall, Harlow

RMT (2013) [accessed 3 January 2013] Welcome to RTM [Online] http://www.rmt.org.uk

Rousseau, D M (1989) Psychological and implicit contracts in organizations, *Employee Responsibilities and Rights Journal*, 2, pp 121–39

Rousseau, D M (1995) *Psychological Contracts in Organizations: Understanding written and unwritten agreements*, Sage, Thousand Oaks, CA

Royal Commission on Trade Unions and Employers' Associations 1965–1968 (1968), Chairman: Lord Donovan, Cmnd. 3623

Salamon, M (2000) *Industrial Relations Theory and Practice*, 4th ed, Prentice Hall, Harlow

Schein, E (1985) *Organizational Culture and Leadership*, Jossey Bass, San Francisco

Sisson, K and Storey, J (2000) *The Realities of Human Resource Management: Managing the employment relationship*, Open University Press, Buckingham

Social Security Act 1986, HMSO, London

Spencer, D (1986) Employee Voice and Employee Retention, *Academy of Management Journal*, 29 (3), pp 488–502

Statutory Maternity Pay Regulations 1986, HMSO, London

Taylor, F W (1911) *Principles of Scientific Management*, Norton, New York

Taylor, S (2008) *People Resourcing*, 4th edn, CIPD, London

The Conduct of Employment Agencies and Employment Business Regulations (2003), HMSO, London

The Financial Times (2013) [accessed 2 February 2013] Companies: The Rise of the Zombies [Online] http://www.ft.com

The Guardian (2012) [accessed 13 December 2013] Comet: More than 6,000 jobs at risk [Online] http://www.guardian.co.uk/technology/2012/nov/01/comet-electrical-goods-jobs-risk

The New York Times (2013) [accessed 23 July 2013] Amazon's Labor Relations Under Scrutiny in Germany [Online] http://www.nytimes.com/2013/03/04/business/global/amazons-labor-relations-under-scrutiny-in-germany.html?pagewanted=all&_r=0

The Telegraph (2011) [accessed 6 November 2012] Obama oil spill commission's final report blames disaster on cost-cutting by BP and partners [Online] http://www.telegraph.co.uk/finance/newsbysector/energy/oilandgas/8242557/Obama-oil-spill-commissions-final-report-blames-disaster-on-cost-cutting-by-BP-and-partners.html

The UK Register of Mediators (2012) [accessed 26 July 2013] What Does Registration Mean? [Online] http://www.ukregisterofmediators.co.uk/what-does-registration-mean/

Thomas, K W (1992) Conflict and negotiation processes in organizations, in Dunnette, M D and Hough, L M (eds) *Handbook of Industrial and Organizational Psychology*, 2nd ed, 3, pp 651–77, Consulting Psychologists Press, Palo Alto, CA

Thomas, M (2011) Global Industrial Relations? Framework agreements and the regulation of international labour standards, *Labour Studies Journal*, 36 (2), pp 269–87

Trade Union and Labour Relations (Consolidation) Act 1992, HMSO, London

Transfer of Undertakings (Protection of Employment) Regulations 2006, HMSO, London

TUC (2001) [accessed 26 July 2013] Bristol City Council: The TUC Time of our lives project [Online] http://www.tuc.org.uk/changingtimes/casestudies_bristol.htm

TUC (2008) [accessed 21 July 2013] Hard Work, Hidden Lives [Online] http://www.vulnerableworkers.org.uk/files/CoVE_full_report.pdf

TUC (2011) [accessed 6 November 2012] Government urged to think again about employment law changes [Online] http://www.tuc.org.uk/workplace/tuc-20317-f0.cfm

Tuckman, B (1965) Developmental sequence in small groups, *Psychological Bulletin*, 63 (6), pp 384–99

UEAPME (2012) [accessed 27 October 2012] About Us [Online] http://www.ueapme.com/spip.php?rubrique1

UKRM (2012) [accessed 22 September 2013] The UK Register of Mediators [Online] Available at http://www.ukregisterofmediators.co.uk/

Ulrich, D (1997) *Human Resource Champions: The next agenda for adding value and delivering results*, Harvard Business School Press, Boston

Unite (2008) [accessed 29 October 2012] Vision and Goals [online] http://www.unitetheunion.org/about_us/vision_and_goals.aspx

USDLC (1994) *Commission on the Future of Worker-Management Relations: Report and recommendations*, United States Departments of Labor and Commerce, Washington, DC, December

Van Wanrooy, B, Bewley, H, Bryson, A, Forth, J, Freeth, S, Stokes, L and Woods, S (2013) *The 2011 Workplace Employment Relations Study: First findings*, Department of Business, Innovation and Skills, London

Varona, F (1996) Relationship between communication satisfaction and organizational commitment in three Guatemalan organizations, *The Journal of Business Communication*, 33 (2), pp 111–40

Varona, F (2002) Conceptualization and management of communication satisfaction and organizational commitment in three Guatemalan organizations, *American Communication Journal*, 5 (2)

Watson v The University of Strathclyde (2011) IRLR 458

Weingart, L and Jehn, K A (2000) Manage intra-team conflict through collaboration, *Blackwell Handbook of Principles of Organizational Behavior*, pp 226–38

Weiss, M (2004) Collective representation in labour law in Germany, *Managerial Law*, 46 (4/5), pp 71–103

West, M A and Farr, J L (1990) Innovation at Work, in West, M A and Farr, J L (eds), *Innovation and Creativity at Work*, Wiley, Chichester

Western Excavating (ECC) Ltd v Sharp [1978] IRLR 27

Wever, K S (1995) Human resource management and organizational strategies in German and US-based companies, *International Journal of HRM*, 6 (3), pp 606–25

Work and Families Act 2006, HMSO, London

INDEX

NB: page numbers in *italic* indicate figures